AMERICAN WEST
LAND OF MANY DREAMS

First English edition published by Colour Library Books Ltd.
© 1984 Illustrations and text: Colour Library Books Ltd.,
    Guildford, Surrey, England.
This edition published by Crescent Books.
Distributed by Crown Publishers, Inc.
h g f e d c b a
Display and text filmsetting by Acesetters Ltd.,
    Richmond, Surrey, England.
Colour separations by Llovet, S.A., Barcelona, Spain.
Printed and bound in Barcelona, Spain by Rieusset and Eurobinder
ISBN 0 517 436396
CRESCENT 1984

AMERICAN WEST
LAND OF MANY DREAMS

Text by Bill Harris

Produced by
TED SMART and DAVID GIBBON

CRESCENT BOOKS
NEW YORK

"It's a thousand miles from the nearest hay, a hundred miles from any firewood, fifty miles from any water fit to drink and less than a foot from hell."

It's the American West. The Wild West. Why in the world would anyone want to live there? In the years after the Civil War, a likely answer from many of the people who did might have been "God made me do it." Many were there in response to what was known as America's "Manifest Destiny," an order from God to go West before the British or the French or the Spanish or even the Russians got their hands on it.

One of the prime movers behind that idea was no less a person than Thomas Jefferson, the country's third President, who had grown up on the wild frontier, which in his day was in Virginia. Though he was possibly the most civilized of any President before or since, he was fascinated by both the romance and the scientific aspects of exploring the West, not to mention that there was a tug at his political heartstrings at the possibility that there might be a convenient route by water across the continent that would put America right in the center of trade between Europe and Asia. And then there were all those treasures, furs and who knows what, just waiting out there for someone bold enough to take them.

One of the first of the men Jefferson gathered around him after his election was a young Army captain, Meriwether Lewis, who the new President signed on as his personal secretary. His major qualification, said Jefferson, was his knowledge of the West. It wasn't long before the two men were dreaming about an expedition to find out what really was out there.

Some people said there was a great river running from east to west and most believed that the Rocky Mountains were nothing more that a high, but narrow, ridge that overlooked the Pacific Ocean on their western side. No matter that Spanish explorers had crossed the southern Rockies and thought otherwise; or that Alexander Mackenzie had crossed the Canadian Rockies in 1793 and had written a book describing in detail what it was like out there.

Our West is different, said the Americans. But they didn't know for sure. What Jefferson did know for sure was that it wasn't "our West." The British, egged on by Mackenzie, were establishing themselves as the dominant fur traders in the Northwest and showed every sign of moving their influence south.

Much of the territory in question belonged to Spain in the 1790s, but the Spaniards had given up on it and in a secret treaty gave the area then called Louisiana to Napoleon in 1800. The French had been in North America about as long as anyone, but their Empire was a shadow of its former self and Napoleon was determined to correct that situation without delay. But he ran into a delay along the way in the form of revolutionary natives in the Caribbean. His army was decimated and he was forced to postpone his occupation of Louisiana, much to the delight of the British Navy who looked at it as a great opportunity.

But Napoleon turned it into an opportunity of his own. Jefferson had already suggested that the United States might be interested in buying New Orleans as a means of keeping the Mississippi River open to American shipping. Napoleon countered with an offer that they could have the whole territory west of the River if they wanted it. The price was $15 million. The territory, south to the Gulf of Mexico, but not including Texas, north to the Great Lakes and west to the Rocky Mountains covered 883,000 square miles. It was more land area than Britain, France and Spain together with Germany, Italy and Portugal thrown in.

"Sold!" said Jefferson and the United States doubled in size.

Napoleon couldn't help smiling. He had raised enough money to rebuild his army and he gave the British a new enemy to think about. The British knew the enemy well. The treaty that ended the American War for Independence had been signed in 1783, just 20 years before.

Though he was a bit surprised when Napoleon made his offer, Jefferson had already authorized Meriwether Lewis to form a party to explore the West and had appointed William Clark as his second in command. Congress had appropriated $2500 to outfit a party of 45 volunteers and the taxpayers were told (along with the British, who were sensitive to such things) that Lewis and Clark and their men were off on a "literary pursuit." They were supplied with everything they might need from $696-worth of "Indian presents" (the biggest item in their budget) to French and Spanish passports before word arrived from Paris that their journey would be through territory claimed by their own government.

The expedition left Illinois on May 14, 1804 and arrived back at St. Louis two years, four months and nine days later.

It was far from a casual junket.

The men had been recruited from frontier Army posts. All were volunteers and, as it happened, all were single men. All except one. Toussaint Chabonneau was a French-Canadian who lived among the Indians in present-day North Dakota. The expedition spent its first winter there and during that time Chabonneau signed on as an interpreter. When they moved out in the spring, Chabonneau's Indian wife, Sacagawea, and their son, at the time less than six-months old, were also part of the company.

Sacagawea, the Bird-woman, was the sister of the chief of the Shoshonis. She had been kidnapped by the Mandans, who sold her to Chabonneau as a slave. Even though he already had two other wives, Chabonneau married the girl, which was a lucky break for Lewis and Clark because their route took them through Shoshoni country which she knew well and where she was well known. Because she had a papoose strapped to her back, other tribes were reassured that this was no war party. None of them would think of taking a young mother off to war. Finally, because she was made of tough stuff, she was stoic about the rough weather and the rough country they faced. That was a life-saving inspiration to the men who would sooner die than give up in the face of conditions that didn't seem to faze a young woman.

Most of the Indians they encountered had never seen a white man before, none had ever seen a black man. Captain Clark provided that novelty for them in the person of his personal slave, a giant of a man named York.

On the hundredth anniversary of their feat, a historian wrote:"York was the observed of all observers, the curiosity of all the party to the red men. He was a negro slave servant to Captain Clark, and the one individual who extracted from the exploration the largest amount of purely physical and superficial enjoyment. His color, kinky hair and size and his prodigious strength were a revelation to the Indians, and he was looked upon as a very god. He was the greatest kind of 'great medicine,' and all the tribes from the mouth of the Missouri to the mouth of the Columbia took particular pains to propitiate his sable majesty, and he was overwhelmed with feminine attentions."

In their journals, Captains Lewis and Clark, both Virginians, treat York matter-of-factly. More than once they reported being able to distract suspicious Indians with the promise of showing them a black man. The Indians, of course, didn't believe what they saw and tried to rub what they thought must be black paint from his body. As proof that York was no hoax, Indians were encouraged to study his scalp through his hair. As for York himself, he seemed to enjoy every minute of it. He told the Indians that he had originally been a wild animal and that Captain Clark had tamed him. To back up his claim, he'd make angry faces and roar, a demonstration Clark wrote "made him more terrible than we wished." The feminine attentions were remembered by a Cayuse Indian woman in Oregon who had been 15 years old when the Lewis and Clark party arrived there. In an interview given on her 110th birthday, the most interesting thing she could remember was "there was a black man."

In his instructions to Lewis, Jefferson had written: "In all your intercourse with the natives, treat them in a most friendly and conciliatory manner...allay all jealousies as to the object of your journey...make them acquainted with the position, extent, character, peacable and commercial disposition of the United States, of our wish to be neighborly, friendly and useful to them."

Everywhere they went, they made it a point to treat the Indians with dignity, a policy that would change in later years. Every encounter began with an invitation to the chiefs to hold a council of peace. The first, which was held on August 2, 1804 at the present site of Council Bluffs, Iowa, set the pattern for most of the others.

Six chiefs of the Oto and Missouri tribes assembled with Captains Lewis and Clark under a tent made of the sail from one of the American keelboats. The ceremony began with a review of a parade of the expedition members, each carrying all his weapons. Then one of the captains made a speech to explain that this was now U.S. territory and that the new White Father had sent out this expedition to learn more of the Red Man and to offer a hand of friendship. Each chief responded to the news in his own way, usually open and friendly, and then it was time for the good part.

Once the speechmaking was over, a peacepipe was passed among them and the Americans handed out gifts of medals and flags, pieces of clothing and special colorful certificates inscribed with the name of the Great White Father and the individual chief who received it. Like the Wizard of Oz, the American Captain explained that what separated leaders from ordinary citizens was often nothing more than a piece of paper and that this particular piece of paper would prove to anyone who could read (and there weren't many of *those* along the banks of the Missouri River!) that the bearer was a true leader of men. Once the ceremonies were over, the chiefs were dazzled by demonstrations of such wonders as a magnet and a spyglass and the most unusual wonder of all (except for York, the black man), an air gun that Lewis had brought along. Then, as a final clincher, a bottle of whiskey was produced and, with a reminder to tell their friends among the other chiefs that these were very special white men, the expedition was ready to go on its way.

Lewis and Clark were sincerely interested in extending a friendly hand to the Indians, but not all the Indians reacted in the same way.

There were no smiling faces waiting them eight weeks

after their first council when they entered the territory of a branch of the Sioux Nation known as the Tetons near the center of present-day South Dakota. The Tetons were known to be hostile, but accepted the invitation to a council and even sent their principal chief to participate. As a safety measure, the Americans chose a sandbar in the middle of the river as the council site and all went well until one of the chiefs appeared to get drunk when the ritual bottle of whiskey was passed. Clark delivered the chiefs to shore as quickly as he could and as he was turning to go back to the protection of the sandbar, the Sioux leader punched him in the chest and told him the gifts were nothing more than cheap junk and that the expedition wasn't going to go any further west.

The riverbank was lined with Sioux braves, but Clark drew his sword and ordered the men who had come with him to go back for help. Lewis, meanwhile, seeing what was happening, unveiled a cannon on the deck of one of the keelboats and ordered every man to take aim with their long rifles on the braves.

It was a tense moment but the chief, by now no longer showing any sign of drunkenness, ordered his men to put down their bows and Clark was free to leave. There was a condition, though. Three of the Indians were to spend the night on one of the boats.

The next morning, the boats were moved upriver closer to the Sioux village and much to the surprise of the Americans, the Indians were downright friendly. Possibly they were impressed by Clark's courage, maybe the cannon had something to do with it. By afternoon, both Lewis and Clark were ceremoniously carried into the village for a feast that featured the greatest delicacy known to the Sioux, roast dog.

That night, other Indians invited themselves to sleep over on one of the boats and the following day the round of dancing and entertainment continued. During the festivities, a slave of the Indians whispered to one of the Americans that this was all a trick and that the expedition would soon be wiped out to the last man. Based on that intelligence, a decision was made to shove off at sunrise. But before they could, some of the Indian guards took hold of the boat's tow cable and their chief, who had invited himself on board for a little ride, announced that they wanted tobacco.

By that point, Clark had had enough. He put the chief ashore and once again turned his cannon on the braves. Then, casually tossing a bag of tobacco in their direction, he ordered the boats to head for midstream and then upstream.

The Indians followed them for a while, but for all intents, the ordeal ended there. And, of course, word went out among other tribes that these Americans weren't easy to bully.

Whatever the reason, the party had no Indian problems at all as they followed the river across the Plains. It allowed them to take more time to observe and record the wonders of this strange land. They collected samples of plant life and swatted mosquitoes. They picked up skeletons and live examples of various animals none of them had ever seen before and they swatted mosquitoes. They collected Indian artifacts from pottery to buffalo robes which would be sent back down the Missouri and then to Washington for delivery to President Jefferson. And they swatted mosquitoes.

By the time the autumn winds eliminated the mosquito problem, they were at a point about dead center of today's North Dakota. They set up winter camp there among the villages of the Mandan and Minitaris. In their journals, the explorers estimated that they had almost 4500 Indian neighbors that winter. There were British trappers there, too, who kept the Americans on edge by circulating rumors among the Indians that the expedition wasn't really on the up and up. The British, who had been running trap lines down from Canada, saw the handwriting on the wall that their days in this territory were numbered and they did all they could to fend off the competition.

But they all had other things to think about. Even the Canadians had never seen a winter like the one they had on the Great Plains in 1804-05. Early in December the temperature dropped to 45 below zero and it didn't warm up much until the end of March. Clark reported that the Missouri froze over solidly enough to support hundreds of buffalo at one time.

By the time spring came, the Indians had told Lewis and Clark what to look for and what to look out for in the country to the west, but they hadn't fully prepared them for the wild country they'd find. The explorers found that out for themselves.

They were in country that no white man had ever seen before. And they began seeing wildlife they had only heard about before. They began seeing moose and antelope and bighorn sheep and as they moved across the high Plains into present-day Montana, they encountered a species they soon learned was best avoided: grizzly bears. In their first encounter with one, they were amazed that the beast charged them after they had pumped four bullets into him. They were even more amazed that he didn't stop charging when three more bullets found their mark and he'd probably have chased them all the way back to St. Louis if a lucky shot, the eighth, hadn't penetrated the animal's skull.

It taught the explorers a little something extra about respecting nature. They saw hundreds of grizzlies after that, but did all they could to keep their distance, using spyglasses to record descriptions, the first ever written by white men. They found another new menace as they approached the Continental Divide: rattlesnakes, thousands of them. But from early April when they left the winter camp until mid-June when they reached the Rocky Mountains, one thing they didn't see was Indians. It's certain that a lot of Indians saw them, but no contact was made and it was the one thing Lewis and Clark wanted more than anything else. The river came down out of the mountains in the form of a spectacular waterfall that caused such a roar the party heard it ten miles away. They obviously needed to go around it and for that they needed horses. They had been told that the Indians in the area had plenty of horses for sale, but if that were the case, they weren't very good at advertising the fact.

It took the white men a month to drag their gear around the falls with a net forward progress of less than 20 miles. They knew they still had a long way to go to reach their destination on the Pacific Ocean and they still had those mountains to cross. Without horses.

They may never have made it of they hadn't stumbled across an old Indian woman and two young girls, the first "aborigines" they had seen since spring. With the help of Sacagawea, they convinced the woman to lead them to the Indian camp where they held a council with their chief, all the while eyeing a herd of some 800 horses. The chief, Cameahwait, was eyeing their Indian guide. It didn't take him long to figure out who she was. Sacagawea was his sister. She had been carried off from this country five years earlier an 11-year-old girl. Now she was a young woman. And she had come home.

Negotiations were laborious. These Indians were Shoshoni, but no one among the explorers except Sacagawea spoke their language. She didn't speak English, nor did her French-speaking husband, Charbonneau. The conversed with each other in the language of the Plains Indians and Charbonneau talked with the Americans through another French-Canadian member of the party. So conversations with the Shoshoni were translated into a different Indian language, then into French and then into English.

But it was worth the trouble. The Shoshoni were familiar with the country to the west and they were willing to sell a couple of horses (the number finally reached more than 30) plus some mules. And though by then it was nearly fall and snowflakes were beginning to reach the high mountain passes, the expedition decided to press on toward the Columbia River. Though they had technically already passed the western boundary of the Louisiana Territory, the American Government had long ago placed a shaky claim on the area to the west known as Oregon, and that had been their goal from the beginning.

Getting there was no fun at all. Game was scarce and they were forced to kill some of their horses for food. The weather went from bad to worse. Fortunately, the Indians they met along the way, especially the Flatheads and Nez Perces, were friendly and helpful. Ironically, their first encounter with the Flatheads was a war party on its way to Shoshoni Country to recover 25 or more horses that had been stolen from them, undoubtedly to restock the herd after selling horses to Lewis and Clark.

By late September, the race against winter was very serious indeed. But they had reached the Columbia River. They left some of their supplies and all their horses with the Nez Perces and took to the water in newly-built canoes. The trip took more than a month, during which they encountered rapids and waterfalls and decidedly unfriendly Indians. But in late October, one of the party sighted Mount Hood off in the distance, a sign that the ocean was near. And then during the first week in November, they spotted the ocean itself. Not a moment too soon, as a violent thunderstorm had been raging for more than ten straight days. The Northwest wasn't fought-over for its climate.

The party spent the rest of the winter in a fort they built just south of the mouth of the Columbia. It wasn't a pleasant winter, but not nearly as cold as it had been out on the Plains. The problem was that it rained every day. There were only 12 days that winter when rain didn't fall, but the sun didn't come out on those days, either. It not only dampened their spirits, but it mildewed their clothing, soaked their gunpowder and made their rheumatism act up.

The Indians, who were familiar with Europeans, weren't a bit friendly, though not troublesome. The party didn't meet any of the traders and trappers who were regulars in the Northwest, probably because the more experienced whites knew better than to go there in the winter.

They were eager to get on with their trip and took advantage of a slight break in the weather to get underway late in March. They should have waited. When they reached the Rockies in early May, they were forced to camp nearly a month because the snow was too deep in the mountain passes.

They did more exploring on the way back, at one point in present-day Montana breaking up into two groups to add to their knowledge of the Yellowstone River. Lewis and some of his men went north into Blackfoot country, a side trip he and others who followed him would live to regret.

They were attacked by a small band of Indians who tried to steal their horses. In the skirmish, Lewis shot and killed one of the Blackfeet. They had never been a particularly friendly tribe, but the killing made them swear to take vengeance on all whites who invaded their territory. The war lasted for decades before the Americans solved the problem by wiping out the Blackfeet and making Montana safe for civilization.

The explorers reunited at the mouth of the Yellowstone and from there went back to St. Louis. The day before they arrived, in September, 1806, they knew they were back in civilized country because they saw cows grazing on the riverbank. It may be the only time in history that seeing a cow was cause for celebration. In spite of their ordeal, only one of the party had died, of what medical historians say was probably appendicitis. Only one had been seriously wounded. Lewis was shot in the leg by a one-eyed scout who seems to have thought he was shooting an elk.

But even though they had read Alexander Mackenzie's book about his expedition across Canada and had talked with Indians and trappers, neither Lewis nor Clark had expected the barriers they encountered. And their published journals didn't gloss over the fact that the American West would be tough to tame. But possibly not too many people read the book. The publisher claimed a final profit of only slightly more than $150 from it. Yet their journey stirred something in the American soul and from the moment they arrived back in St. Louis the dreams of restless Americans turned west.

John Colter, who had gone west with Lewis and Clark, didn't want to go back to civilization and stayed behind to become a trapper and explorer. His tales of the Great Salt Land and the wonders of the area that since became Yellowstone National Park and the awesome beauty of the Grand Tetons to the south were written off by many as tall tales, but served as a lure to other adventuresome spirits who followed him.

In the next several years dozens of hardy souls set out across the Plains and into the mountains. Captain Zebulon Pike led an official expedition into the mountains of present-day Colorado. Further north at least two major fur trading posts were established, one in 1807 by Manuel Lisa at the mouth of Montana's Bighorn River and another in 1810 by Andrew Henry on the other side of the Continental Divide near the Snake River.

But American fur trade didn't get really serious until 1810 when a New Yorker got into the act and gave the West a profit motive.

John Jacob Astor was his name. He was a German immigrant who made good trading with fur trappers from the northern reaches of New York State. As he became more successful, he spread his net further away and became a good customer of the trappers in French Canada. Many of them were bringing furs to Montreal from the far west, often from territory claimed by the United States. Because he was importing from Canada, though, he had to pay duty on the furs before he could get them to New York. The Louisiana Purchase made him determined to avoid that extra fee. Lewis and Clark showed him that it would be humanly possible.

The principal market for furs in those days was in China and Japan and Astor thought he could reach his ultimate customers more easily if he shipped direct across the Pacific, and to accomplish that he dispatched not one, but two westward expeditions in 1810. One went by sea from New York bound for Oregon via Cape Horn and the other overland. Neither party had an easy time of it, but by late summer in 1811 Astor had about 100 men working for him in a new fort at the mouth of the Columbia River, a fort he modestly called Astoria.

British fur traders had already established outposts further up the coast, but Astor still had a marketing advantage over them. The men who ran things from England had a hard and fast rule that any furs sent out to Asia from their North American posts had to go through London first.

But Astor wasn't out of the woods yet. While his men were getting their act together, the United States declared war on Great Britain. The British had a warship in the Pacific, but the Americans didn't and that left the Astorians high and dry.

Being good businessmen, they decided not to wait for the British guns to arrive and sold the place to the Canadian-based North West Company. By the time the smoke cleared and the war ended, the American-Canadian border was clearly established but the Oregon territory was declared an international zone, a status that lasted until a compromise was struck in 1846. Through those years, men who ventured west were mainly trappers and spies for the various countries who wanted to keep an eye on the other countries with interests in the American West. They went disguised as writers or hunters or curiosity-seekers but they didn't fool anybody. The Canadian trappers and the American fur hunters kept expanding meanwhile and competition among them was fierce. But there was plenty of wealth to go around and, except for the

beavers, the only real losers were the Indians. In Canada, the Hudson's Bay Company made it illegal to supply Indians with liquor. But there was nothing wrong with dispensing firewater outside British territory and liquor became a principal weapon in the rivalry among the entrepreneurs who weren't above a little calumny, either. Systematically they managed to turn tribe against tribe and in less than 30 years turned friendly Indians into hostile Indians, a condition that would haunt the descendants of all of them.

Then, in 1831, religion became a reason to head for the West. Some migrating Iroquois had told the Flathead Indians that the white man had brought them good medicines back East and that medicine was the Word of God. Intrigued, they sent a delegation to St. Louis to find out more about this thing. It seems strange that no one had thought of it before, but their plea didn't fall on deaf ears and two years later, the Methodist Episcopal Church officially formed a party of missionaries to take the Word west. A year later, an interdenominational group did the same thing. Scores of independent ministers and their families ventured west at the same time but though they found the Indians very much in need of what they had to give, they didn't find the missionary business too rewarding. The problem, it seems, was that they were all Protestants. What the Flatheads had heard about were the French Catholic priests who wore long black robes. These people wore frock coats and neckties and derby hats and somehow didn't seem to be talking about the same Great Spirit. But the missionaries had gone west at great expense. If the Indians weren't buying what they had to sell, they'd have to find someone who would. Many went back home to round up more recruits, raised more money and then headed west again with followers they claimed were also "missionaries," but who in reality were settlers.

Back East in the first quarter of the nineteenth century, the American Dream was beginning to look a little shoddy to many people. New England had become overrun with factories that produced all sorts of modern conveniences but didn't pay wages big enough to let the workers buy what they produced. Cities were beginning to show signs of decay. Farmers found their markets shrinking and competition increasing as the midwest began producing more and more food. Most people were either immigrants themselves or could easily trace their roots back to men and women who had come to America looking for opportunity. And opportunity was still here. It was waiting to be seized by anyone bold enough to go west. And there were plenty of people telling them about it. Washington Irving was one. The most popular writer of his day had written in 1836 about the adventures of establishing Astoria on the Oregon coast, a writing project carefully orchestrated by John Jacob Astor himself. And then a year later, Irving produced another bestseller based on the diaries of a fur trader named Benjamin Bonneville.

The second book was well-timed. When it appeared, the country was in a depression that had caused foreclosures on a lot of mortgages. To the affected people a land without banks and with plenty of wide-open spaces was very tempting indeed.

But the route to the west didn't have any arrowed signs saying "Utopia – 2,000 miles." Though a lot of people had already trekked that way and many had carefully recorded the landmarks along the way, there was no "official" route. That came after 1842 when a progressive Government dispatched J.C. Fremont to blaze such a trail for future emigrants. When he got back in the fall of 1842, he was whisked off to Washington where his official report was published and eagerly grabbed up by would-be emigrants who had been carefully cultivated by one of the greatest public relations campaigns in the history of the country.

The Oregon Territory was still officially an international zone. In the end it could still become British. But the pamphleteers found an advantage in that. Britain was still our enemy, they said. The scares of the Revolution and the short war of 1812 made that an easy idea to sell. The continuing depression made this place seem like a perfect way to get out from under and start all over again. And then there was that Manifest Destiny. As a God-fearing people, Americans responded enthusiastically to the idea that God himself had mandated that the West should be tamed and settled, preferably by Americans. The basic idea behind it all was Washington's interest in making sure that all of the West, Oregon as well as the Spanish Southwest, would eventually become part of the United States. The best way to accomplish that, short of war, was to fill the land with Americans.

Thousands had gone before, but the real push west began in the spring of 1843. Near the end of May, nearly a thousand people gathered at Independence, Mo., after having packed all their belongings into great wagons. On the day they left, a young lawyer with special interest in keeping "haughty Albion" from taking over the West, wrote that this was "one of the most arduous and important trips undertaken in modern times."

He reported that there were over one hundred wagons carrying 260 men, 130 women and 610 children. Behind them trailed more than 5,000 cattle.

The trip was arduous, to be sure, but not as bad as any of them had expected. They started out with no special leaders or organization, just a bunch of people all going in the same direction at the same time. But not much time went by before they realized they had to change all that. Guards were appointed, advance scouts sent out to select camp sites, and rules of conduct were established to make sure everybody was working together toward a common goal. Some of the party drowned, some died of natural causes, but they arrived in the Oregon Territory relatively unscathed at about the same time as winter arrived.

Looking back on it, many said, the trip from the East to Independence was the hard part. From there on it could almost be called fun. And in a letter to the New York Herald, one of them reported that he had even made money on the trip because he sold the wagon that had carried his family across the Prairie and up over the mountains.

The following year, 1,400 more emigrants made the trip.

Of all the things that were written, either to encourage more people to go or simply to record what life in a wagon train was like, the most fascinating came along in 1876, 33 years after the fact, by Jesse Applegate, who had been put in charge of half of the 1843 train, the one with the cattle in tow. He chose to describe a typical day:

"It is four o'clock A.M.; the sentinels on duty have discharged their rifles, a signal that the hours of sleep are over. Every wagon and tent is pouring forth its night tenants, and slow-kindling smoke begins to rise and float away in the morning air. Sixty men start from the corral, spreading as they make through the vast herd of cattle and horses that make a semicircle around the encampment, the most distant perhaps two miles away.

"...In about an hour five thousand animals are close up to the encampment and the teamsters are busy selecting

their teams and driving them inside the corral to be yoked. The corral is a circle one hundred yards deep, formed with wagons connected strongly with each other; the wagon in the rear being connected with the wagon in front by its tongue and ox chains.

"...From six to seven o'clock is a busy time; breakfast is to be eaten, the tents struck, the wagons loaded and the teams yoked and brought up in readiness to be attached to their respective wagons. All know when, at seven o'clock, the signal sounds to march, that those not ready to take their proper places in the line of march must fall to the dusty rear for the day.

"There are 60 wagons. They have been divided into 15 divisions or platoons of four wagons each, and each platoon is entitled to lead in its turn. The leading platoon today will be the rear one tomorrow, and will bring up the rear unless some teamster, through indolence or negligence, has lost his place in the line and is condemned to that uncomfortable post.

"It is within ten minutes of seven. The corral but now a strong barricade is everywhere broken, the teams being attached to the wagons. The women and children have taken their places in them. The pilot stands ready, in the midst of his pioneers and aides, to mount and lead the way. Ten or fifteen young men, not on duty today, form another cluster. They are ready to start on a buffalo hunt and are well mounted and well armed.

"...It is on the stroke of seven. The rush to and fro, the cracking of whips, the loud commands to the oxen and what seemed to be the inextricable confusion of the last ten minutes has ceased. Fortunately, everyone has been found and every teamster is at his post. The clear notes of a trumpet sound in the front; the pilot and his guards mount their horses and the leading divisions of the wagons move out of the encampment and take up the line of march. The rest fall into their places with the precision of clockwork until the spot so lately full of life sinks back into that solitude that seems to reign over the broad plain and rushing river.

"...It is with the hunters we shall briskly canter toward the bold but smooth and grassy bluffs that bound the broad valley, for we are not yet in sight of the grander but less beautiful scenery of Chimney Rock, Court House and other bluffs so nearly resembling giant castles and palaces, where the Platte passes through the highlands near Laramie. ...We have reached the top of the bluff and have turned to view the wonderful panorama spread before us. To those who have not been on the Platte, my powers of description are wholly inadequate to convey an idea of the vast extent and grandeur of the picture and the rare beauty and distinctness of the detail.

"We are full six miles away from the line of march and though everything is dwarfed by distance, it is seen distinctly. The caravan has been in motion about two hours and is now as widely extended as a prudent regard for safety will permit. First, near the bank of a shining river is a company of horsemen. They seem to have found an obstruction, for the main body has halted while three of four ride rapidly along the bank of the creek. They are hunting for a favorable crossing for the wagons. While we are watching, they have succeeded. It has apparently required no work to make it possible, for all but one of the party have passed on, and he has raised a flag, no doubt a signal to the wagons to steer their course to where he stands. The leading teamster sees him, though he is yet two miles off, and steers his course directly toward him, the rest of the wagons following directly in his track.

"They form a line three-quarters of a mile in length. Some of the teamsters ride upon the front of the wagons, some march alongside their teams. Scattered along the line, companies of women are taking exercise on foot, gathering bouquets of the rare and beautiful flowers that line the way. Near them stalks a stately greyhound or an Irish wolf dog, apparently proud of keeping watch and ward over his master's wife and children. Next comes a band of horses. Two or three men or boys follow them, the docile and sagacious animals scarcely needing their attention. ...Not so with the large herd of horned beasts that brings up the rear, lazy, selfish and unsocial.

"...The pilot, by measuring the ground and timing the speed of the wagons and the walk of his horses, has determined the rate of each, so as to enable him to select the nooning place as nearly as the requisite grass and water can be found at the end of five hours' travel of the wagons. ...He and his pioneers are at the nooning place an hour in advance of the wagons, which time is spent in preparing convenient watering places and digging little wells near the bank of the Platte, as the teams are not unyoked, but simply turned loose from the wagons. A corral is not formed at noon, but the wagons are drawn up in columns, four abreast, the leading wagon of each platoon on the left. ...This brings friends together at noon as well as at night.

"Today an extra session of the council is being held to settle a dispute that does not admit of delay, between a proprietor and a young man who had undertaken to do a man's service on the journey for bed and board. ...This high court, from which there is no appeal, will define the rights of each party.

"At one o'clock, the bugle had sounded and the caravan has resumed its westward journey. It is in the same order, but the evening is far less animated than the morning march. A drowsiness has fallen apparently on man and beast, teamsters drop asleep on their perches and even when walking by their teams and the words of command are now addressed to the slowly creeping oxen in the soft tenor of women and the piping treble of children.

"A little incident breaks the monotony of the march: An emigrant's wife, whose state of health has caused Doctor Whitman to travel near the wagon for the day, is now taken with a violent illness. The Doctor has had the wagon driven out of the line, a tent pitched and a fire kindled. Many conjectures are hazarded in regard to this mysterious proceeding and as to why the lone wagon is to be left behind.

"And we, too, must leave it, hasten to the front and note the proceedings. For the sun is now getting low in the west and the painstaking pilot is standing ready to conduct the train in the circle which he has previously measured and marked out and which will form the invariable fortification for the night. The leading wagons follow him so nearly around the circle that but a wagon length separates them. Each wagon follows in its track, the rear closing in on the front, until its tongue and ox chain will perfectly reach from one to the other. So accurate is the measure and perfect the practice that the hindmost wagon of the train always precisely closes the gateway. As each wagon is brought into position it is dropped from its team (the teams being inside the circle), the team is unyoked and the yokes and chains are used to connect each wagon strongly with that in its front.

"Within ten minutes from the time the leading wagon halted, the barricade is formed, the teams unyoked and driven out to pasture. Everyone is busy preparing fires

of buffalo chips to cook the evening meal, pitching tents and otherwise preparing for the night. This night, there are anxious watchers for the absent wagon, for there are many matrons who may be afflicted like its inmate before the journey is over. ...But as the sun goes down the absent wagon rolls into camp, the bright speaking face and cherry look of the doctor, who rides in advance, declare without words that all is well and that both mother and child are comfortable.

"It is not yet eight o'clock when the first watch is to be set; the evening meal is just over and the corral, now free from the intrusion of the cattle or horses, has groups of children scattered over it. ...Before a tent near the river, a violin makes lively music and some youths and maidens have improvised a dance upon the green. In another quarter, a flute gives its mellow and melancholy notes to the still night air. ...It has been a prosperous day, more than 20 miles have been accomplished of this great journey.

"But time passes. The watch has been set up for the night, the council of old men has been broken up...the flute has whispered its last lament...the dancers have dispersed. ...All is hushed and repose from the fatigues of the day, save the vigilant guard and the wakeful leader, who still has cares upon his mind that forbid sleep. He hears the 10 o'clock relief taking his post and the 'All's Well' report of the returned guard. ...The last care of the day removed and the last duty performed, he, too, seeks the rest that will enable him to go through the same routine tomorrow."

Generally speaking, families who went west in those early wagon trains didn't suffer a whole lot more than people who explore the National Parks in motorhomes and trailers today. They had much less trouble finding a place to camp for the night, at the very least. Many didn't make it and the trails were marked by the graves of the very young and the very old and the occasional careless who preferred to make their own rules. But even the 1846 Donner party, often cited as the most harrowing of all pioneer experiences, lost only 40 of its 87 members. They had taken some bad advice and a wrong turn on the way to California. They were forced to cross more than 500 miles of desert and were trapped in the mountains when the winter snows hit and, according to most accounts, turned to cannibalism to stay alive until spring.

But if the pre-Civil War pioneers had a relatively easy trans-continental adventure, there was plenty of wild adventure on the Plains and in the mountains and there were men who thrived on it. Kit Carson was one. He had grown up in Missouri and lived in the Southwest and California before signing on as a guide for the 1842 Fremont expedition. Fremont was so impressed, he hired Carson to guide them into California the following summer. The official reports of both expeditions guaranteed that Kit Carson would live forever as the first real hero of the Wild West. He fought Indians with one hand and wild animals with the other, according to Fremont, while his mind was occupied with outsmarting the wily Mexican. And if Fremont's reports didn't do enough to build the man's reputation, cheap novels and magazines back East pumped it up even further. It impressed the great General William Tecumseh Sherman, who couldn't resist a little name-dropping in 1849 when he wrote that he had met Kit Carson in person. He was very impressed, he said, by "...the man who had achieved such feats of daring among the wild animals of the Rocky Mountains and the still wilder Indians of the Plains."

Carson himself wasn't quite as impressed by all those stories, although he was well-aware of them. One probably true story about him is that he once led a daring raid into an Apache camp to rescue a captive white woman. When they got there, the Indians had escaped and the woman was dead, but near her body was a paperback novel whose plot centered around the same adventure he was experiencing right then. But the outcome was different. In the fictional account, the Indians were all dead and the woman had melted into the arms of her brave rescuer, a lone hero named Christopher Carson. The one everyone called "Kit."

Kit Carson was a Mountain Man, one of hundreds who went up into the Rocky Mountains in the 1830s in search of adventure and beaver skins. The exploits attributed to Carson could have applied to almost any of them, but most are forgotten now, having passed out of the world as silently as they passed through it. Some, like Jim Bridger, who eventually opened a trading post and earned a comfortable living, when he wasn't off again in search of more adventure, and John Colter have left their names on the incredibly beautiful landscape they were first to see.

Colter went back East and retired at 35 in St. Louis. His last adventure, and one that sent him back to civilization, nearly cost him his life. He and his partner had wandered too far north into Blackfoot country. The Indians captured them, killed Colter's companion and, just for the fun of it, took all Colter's clothes and told him to run for his life. They, of course, intended to run after him with their spears and bows and arrows. Miraculously, he managed to outrun them and finally escaped by jumping into a river and swimming underwater into the hidden entrance of a beaver lodge. It was a trick the Indians should never have been fooled by, but it worked and Colter vowed not to push his luck again. On the other hand, civilization wasn't kind to him. He lived in retirement for three years and died at 38, a ripe old age for a Mountain Man at that.

They came down out of the mountains once a year for their annual rendezvous. The site was arranged the year before by the people who ran wagon trains back to St. Louis and were the only customers the Mountain Men had. The wagons would arrive from the East loaded with tobacco and whiskey, food and clothing, guns and powder and other things considered to be the necessities of a simple life. The goods were sold at high prices, the trappers' furs were bought at low prices and during the long negotiations, the men from the mountains took advantage of the opportunity to get drunk, to get into fights, to tell tall tales and to look over the Indian women most of them would eventually buy so they'd have companionship and maid service during the next trapping season.

The Mountain Men were a scruffy-looking bunch. Their clothes were made of animal skins, their hair and beards were matted with bear grease. Their manners were worse. But they knew how to survive and they showed the people who followed them just how it was done.

An exception to the rule was Jedediah Smith, who read from the Bible each day and slavishly followed its teaching. Believing that cleanliness is next to Godliness, he also made it a point to take a bath every day, something not many people back in the civilized East did, and he shaved every day. One day early in his career he was badly mauled by a grizzly bear who left him with a horribly mangled ear and from that day on, he never wore his hair short again. But, except for that, he looked as little like a Mountain Man as any man could look. Even his clothes were clean. But he was like the others in terms of bravery and a thirst for adventure. He had gone west in 1822 to join an organized company of trappers along with the likes of Jim Bridger, Bill Sublette, who would discover a shortcut for the Oregon Trail, and David Jackson, whose headquarters in a

Wyoming valley would give his name to one of the most wonderfully beautiful spots in the entire West. Before he was killed by Comanches in the Southwest in 1831, Jed Smith had explored more of the West than any man, possibly of any race. In the process, he discovered South Pass, a 25-mile-wide valley running east to west through the mountains. It was an easy route to California, though deserts lay between it and the Pacific. But he explored those, too, and left behind valuable advice for pioneers who followed him. Another way that Jedediah Smith differed from the usual run of Mountain Men was that he could write. And he wrote plenty about all he saw in Spanish California, in British Vancouver, in Mexican Santa Fe and just about everywhere in between.

The writings of men like Smith served as valuable guides to people planning to relocate in the West, but readers in the East began looking for more than territorial descriptions and the heroics of man against nature. One place they got what they wanted was in the *National Police Gazette*, which in the 1870s began telling its readers about a young fellow down in New Mexico named William Bonny. Folks called him Billy The Kid, and really smart folks made it a point to call him that from a distance. The Kid was a killer. He had, they said, a notch in his gun for each of his 21 years and the only time he smiled was when he was killing someone, which was often enough that anyone who didn't know better would think he had a sunny disposition. The Police Gazette and other papers reported with a straight face that The Kid lived in a palace out in the New Mexican desert surrounded by women he had kidnapped, but who nevertheless were quite content with an occasional snarl from his thin lips. He was a snappy dresser, they reported, almost always appearing in a black outfit decorated with jewels and silver bells. Dime novels added to his image as a killer, a rustler, a despoiler of young women, a horse thief and an all-round evil young man. In 1881, a writer in the Chicago Tribune threw up his hands at trying to chronicle all of The Kid's evils, but while he was at it, he managed to take some verbal shots at some other characters, too:

"How many men he killed, how many cattle he stole, how many deeds of daring deviltry and cruelty he perpetrated will probably never be known until the dark deeds of cowboys, congressmen, governors, thieves, law-makers, law-breakers are laid bare to the world."

Poor Billy! Fortunately, he had been dead for a month when that was written and never knew that some day he'd be mentioned in the same sentence with congressmen, governors and law-makers. He'd have been more impressed if he had lived until 1903 when a melodrama about his life gave him a whole new image. He was more to be pitied than censured, said the playwright. He was a lad whose father killed his mother and then set him up to be arrested for it. As the action unfolds, Billy the fugitive becomes something of a Robin Hood, helping everybody but the evil rich. The play was a hit on Broadway and road companies played to packed houses right up to the First World War. In the 1920s, The Kid was the subject of several books that took their basic story line from the play and then in 1930, Johnny Mack Brown, a clean-cut guy if there ever was one, played the title role in MGM's motion picture, *The Saga of Billy The Kid*. Thirty years later, Marlon Brando recreated the character, a little less clean-cut, but still lovable, in the film, *One-Eyed Jacks*.

The truth is, Billy The Kid was neither Johnny Mack Brown nor Marlon Brando. His mother outlived his father and nobody ever had an unkind word for his stepfather. When he was arrested in Las Vegas near the end of his career, a local reporter said:

"He did look human...(but) he looked and acted a mere boy. He is about five feet, eight inches tall, slightly built and lithe, weighing about 140; a frank, open countenance, looking like a schoolboy with the traditional silky fuzz on his upper lip; clear blue eyes with a roguish snap about them; light hair and complexion. He is, in all, quite a handsome-looking fellow, the only imperfection being two prominent front teeth slightly protruding like squirrel's teeth."

The Kid's first killing, at least the first anyone knows of, was in the summer of 1877 when he pumped some hot lead through the apron and into the stomach of Windy Cahill, a blacksmith in Fort Grant, Arizona Territory. He was caught right away and put in jail right away, but he escaped right away and was next heard from in New Mexico where he was identified as part of a roving band of horse thieves.

From there he seems to have made a turn away from his wicked ways and took a job as a cowboy on a ranch in Southern New Mexico that was part of a string of outfits backed by the powerful John Chisum of Texas. At the time a local combine of cattle barons was trying to take over the whole country and had most of the small ranchers in the area indebted to them financially. Billy The Kid's boss put himself in the position of defending the smaller operators and the first of the great Western range wars got underway. Lots of men were killed, including The Kid's boss and later the sheriff, a killing credited to Billy himself. As the war raged on, local newsmen noticed that whenever someone died, it was usually in Billy's presence. No one actually accused him publicly, but when the war eventually ended in favor of the local entrepreneurs, Billy The Kid felt it would be healthier to head north.

It wasn't until he got out of town that people began saying out in the open that The Kid was an outlaw. Their proof was that he and his friends had stolen some horses to make their getaway and in the process had killed the man who had been watching them.

He became known as a horse thief after that and did, indeed, make a fair living selling stolen horses in Texas. Then he started a new career. He had indirectly worked for John Chisum during the range war, but because his boss had been killed and he had made such an abrupt departure, he had never been paid for his efforts or for the risk of his young life. Chisum owed him back pay, he reasoned. But rather than ask for the money, he took it on himself to take some of Chisum's cattle off the open range.

After a brief interlude, during which he had been arrested and taken back to New Mexico for his involvement in the range war, and then escaped again, he killed another man he suspected of having been sent by Chisum to kill him.

Toward the end of 1880, a posse caught up with The Kid and caught him red-handed with some stolen cattle. The sheriff, Pat Garrett, threw the book at him and ordered him to stand trial for the murder of the previous sheriff. He was found guilty and sentenced to be hanged. But with the help of some sympathetic citizens, he managed to escape and cheated the hangman. In the process, he killed his two guards, which outraged the local press and made Sheriff Garrett furious. When he managed to track The Kid down in less than a month, he put an end to the saga with a single bullet in Billy The Kid's head.

Pat Garrett, many said, was a tool of the big cattle barons. It may or may not have been true. But what was,

indeed, true was that John Chisum was one of the most powerful men in New Mexico and he didn't even live there. And there was some speculation that Billy The Kid might have lived to kill again if he hadn't taken to stealing Chisum's cattle.

Cattle ranchers are more a part of the story of the Old West than just about any other type. Texans like Richard King and Mifflin Kenedy were already pioneering the business when the first wagon trains arrived in Oregon. Ranchers from Mexico had tried raising cattle and horses in Southern Texas, but by the 1830s, bandits, hostile Indians and new American settlers had driven them back to Mexico. They left in such a hurry, they didn't bother to take all their horses or any of their cattle. When King first saw the territory, there were thousands of wild horses and tens of thousands of cattle that had adapted through the process of natural selection to not only survive, but to thrive in this near-desert country.

There was only one problem. There was no way to get the cattle to market and walking them a thousand miles was a chancey business. King and Kenedy, who had gotten rich operating riverboats on the Rio Grande, spent their early years as ranchers acquiring land. The ranch they created, still in business and still the biggest in the West, made them rich beyond their wildest dreams.

They didn't ship much cattle at first, except to thin weaker strains from their herd or for sale locally at very low prices, but spent their energies developing a tougher-than-ever longhorn and improving the breed of horses that would be so important to make the cattle business thrive. In fact, it began to look for a while there like cattle would become a secondary product in the King operation because their horse-breeding business was immense, even by Texas standards.

But when the Civil War ended, everything changed. Railroads began to move west, cities in the North mushroomed and the demand for meat mushroomed, too. The soldiers who went out onto the Plains to solve the Indian problem became a market for beef and the Indians they consigned to reservations needed to be fed, too. The great white hunters were systematically destroying the buffalo herds and unless the West was going to be populated by vegetarians, a good substitute was needed. The Texas longhorn filled the bill. They were tough enough to walk themselves to market and with the building of the Atchison, Topeka and Santa Fe Railroad in 1868, the market was as close as southern Kansas.

Thousands of cattle made the march and the drama of the cattle drives fired everyone's imagination. There were established farms between Texas and Kansas, but the ranchers just marched over them, making the farmers very hostile, indeed. To many, that just added to the danger and that added to the fun. The land itself was hostile and guys like Billy The Kid were lurking along the trails waiting to steal a few steers. Yet for all the danger and potential for excitement, the average cattle drive was probably no more dangerous than driving a truck across the country today.

Some 200 herds made the trip every year. Each herd had about 2,500 head of cattle in the care of about a dozen cowboys. They took along five or six horses for each man and the company was followed by a supply wagon, remembered by fans of Western movies as the "chuck" wagon. Assuming there were no unusual problems, a herd could move as far as 15 miles in a day. The average cost per steer for the whole trip averaged out to about 50 cents, a good deal cheaper than any other means of transportation. It was well-worth the trouble. A steer was worth about three dollars if it were sold in Texas. It could bring $20 at the railhead, not a bad return on a 50-cent investment, even better when you consider it cost two dollars a head to raise them in the first place. Profits were so good, in fact, that even though Richard King estimated that rustlers had made off with more than a million dollars worth of his steers in a five-year period, he was making too much money to keep on reinvesting it in land and livestock, and became the owner of a dozen other businesses from railroads to newspapers.

The cowboys who led the steers to market knew the trails well and always knew where the next available water would be. Those places became the established campsites. Today, those spots are still the center of activity for the people who live out on the prairie. The old wells have been taken over as sites for roadside stores that sell gas for the pickup trucks everyone in the West seems to own. But they're something more than gas stations. They're general stores, saloons, meat markets, dance halls and motels, all under a single roof. On Friday nights people gather there from miles around to restock their larders and to recharge their mental batteries with a little gossip, a little story-telling, a lot of companionship. They're following a tradition the cowboys before them established and loved.

The best-known of all the trails north from Texas was the old Chisholm Trail beginning at the Red River and running across Indian territory into Kansas. The trail had been blazed by Jesse Chisholm, a Cherokee Indian who supplied beef to the Army posts out on the Plains. At the other end was a little town called Abilene, Kansas, a place the cowboys put on the map.

When the cowpunchers got there and the cattle were sold, they collected their pay of about $30 for each month's work. It was a fortune to them and there were plenty of ways to spend it in Abilene. There were saloons, for instance; lots of them. And a man does get thirsty on the hot dusty trail. If they were looking for a fight to let off a little steam, that was easy. Most cowboys had roots in the deep South, having come west from Georgia after the Civil War. The Abilene city fathers made it a point to recruit marshalls who had seen service in the Union Army. All of them had deep scars from the war. The result was that it was much easier to find a fight than to avoid one in Kansas in the 1880s.

But the fighting, drinking and carousing was all part of the fun. The rest was no fun at all. If wind, rain, dust and ornery critters made a cowboy's life hard, there were other irritations, too, not the least of them Indians. Before the longhorn, there were buffalo, and the cattle drives went straight across the traditional buffalo hunting grounds that had sustained the Indians for generations. But the tradition had obviously seen its day.

Back East, buffalo robes were all the rage, almost as popular as beaver hats had been and, like the beaver before them, the great American bison became a cash crop worth just about any hardship. But killing bison was a whole lot easier than sloshing through icy water to trap beaver. The buffalo hunters worked together in groups of ten or more with heavy rifles and wagon-loads of ammunition. A good hunter could kill as many as 50 of the huge beasts in a day and their heavy rifles allowed them to do it from a distance. Once they had killed off a herd, they moved on in their wagons to the next herd. Hide wagons followed them and skinners stripped off the hides, leaving the carcasses to rot in the sun.

It was a bloody business and the men who played the game were tough characters. They attracted others like them who played different games. Poker players, dance hall girls, conmen and prostitutes poured in to get their share of the huge profits. The buffalo camps were boom towns where anything could be had for the right price.

Tales of adventure on the Plains lured other white men there and it soon became great sport for amateur hunters to fire into buffalo herds from passing trains, the railroads having promoted the "sport" to sell more tickets. It didn't take long for them to decimate the buffalo herds. Or for the Indians to react.

It has been estimated that in 1803 when the Louisiana Territory became the United States, there were some 30 million buffalo roaming the Plains. The same estimate puts the Indian population at about 200,000. In the ten years beginning in 1870, white men killed buffalo at the rate of about a million a year. Indians were harder to kill.

Some of them tried to extend the hand of friendship, but as Francis Parkman, whose articles in the Boston-based *Knickerbocker Magazine* lured thousands to the West, said privately, "...this country is so beautiful that settlements and towns will soon have to drive out the Indians." He wrote in one of his articles that "the Indians could scarcely believe that the earth contained such a multitude of white men. Their wonder is now giving way to indignation and the result, unless valiantly guarded against, may be lamentable in the extreme." Those words were written in 1846. On New Year's Day, 1891, lamentation was the word of the day for the Red Man. The Indian "problem" was declared officially over.

The problem probably began with the first white trappers who used the Indians to fight their competitive battles for them. It continued all through the 19th century with tales of horror on both sides as the Indians fought a desperate, but losing battle against the sheer numbers of whites who had decided that God wanted them to farm the land, to kill buffalo, to change the course of rivers and to cleanse the world of savages.

The last great holdouts were the Sioux: proud, fierce fighters who had once ranged over territory that today encompasses North and South Dakota, Wyoming, Montana and Nebraska. Ironically, it was the first tribe to show any hostility to the Lewis and Clark expedition. Their final fight was led by the great chief Sitting Bull.

It began on the Fourth of July, 1876, the hundredth birthday of the American nation, when the Sioux nation met the U.S. Cavalry on the banks of the Little Big Horn River in southern Montana. Sitting Bull was given credit for the overwhelming defeat of the white men, but he gave credit to a little Manifest Destiny of his own. The man was a mystic. It was said that he could communicate with animals and that he could see the future in his dreams. Before the battle of Little Big Horn, he had gone into a trance and envisioned the white man's soldiers humiliated in defeat. Whether his prophecy actually came true or whether it gave his braves the extra edge of courage to make it come true is something none of us will ever know. But the whole country soon knew that the Seventh Cavalry, commanded by General George A. Custer, had been wiped out. Historians say it would never have happened if Custer had been a better soldier. Sitting Bull said the soldiers killed and taken prisoner were the special gift of the Sun God. His followers, who had seen Custer's strategy and found it easy to defeat him, chose to believe their victory was a Divine gift. They believed in Sitting Bull, who had shown his incredible bravery as a young man by marching into the thick of enemy fire in an early battle with the Bluecoats, sat down in the center of a field and lit up his pipe. Though bullets whizzed around him, he didn't move on until the pipe had been smoked.

No bullets touched him and he survived to repeat the act in other battles. It never failed to impress the braves. Or the Bluecoats.

But if the Sun God talked to Sitting Bull through the birds and beasts, he was also good at giving practical advice. After the slaughter at Little Big Horn, he knew that the war was far from won. He had told his men not to take the soldiers' guns or other equipment, but they did and in a short time the Americans counterattacked, wiping out an Indian village and taking back the captured goods. Later still, Sitting Bull was lured into a powwow to discuss transferring him and his followers to a reservation. Push came to shove during the meeting and it ended up with a two-day gun battle that left the Sioux badly mauled. Meanwhile, other Sioux, knowing that they were fighting a losing battle, signed a treaty that gave the Americans the Black Hills of South Dakota and all the territory around them; land that earlier American treaties had reserved for the Indians. During the ceremony, Chief Crazy Horse, who the Americans decided wasn't to be trusted, was ordered locked up. In the scuffle that followed when he resisted, he was stabbed and killed.

Sitting Bull wisely broke off the fight and moved his people into Canada where they had been guaranteed protection by England's Queen Victoria. He got his protection, but like the Americans, the British were not at all generous in feeding the flock. Hunting was poor and many of the Indians starved. They were homesick, too, and in 1881, three years after they went north, Sitting Bull led his people back down across the border and surrendered them to the Indian agents at Fort Buford, North Dakota. But he never bowed his head to them. "This land I have under my feet is mine again," he told them. "I never sold it and I never gave it to anybody." Sitting Bull was not a man who gave up.

The Americans kept him under lock and key for two years. Then he was released in the custody of a theatrical producer, who took him on a national tour billed as "The Slayer of General Custer." One of the impressive people he met on the tour was Annie Oakley, who was as handy with a rifle as any girl had ever been.

The tour began in 1884. He made others later, but by 1887, he had retired from show business and gone back to lead what was left of his people. Things went from bad to worse for the old chief, but he did manage to get more favorable treaties for them. Then in 1889 a Paiute brave had a new vision. The dead would return and bring the buffalo with them, he told his followers, and the white man would disappear in their wake. A whole new religion sprang up around him, and he created a ritual that would help them share the vision. Few of the tribes left in the West weren't affected by this new phenomenon the whites called "the ghost dance religion." Though one of its basic tenets was that there should be no more fighting, many followers started wearing shirts they said were bulletproof. That made the whites edgy again. Then it was rumored that Sitting Bull was behind it all and before long a warrant was issued for his arrest.

The Indian agents weren't crazy. They knew that any attempt to put the chief into jail would be something close to a suicidal act. But fortunately, the reservations were kept peaceful by Indians who had been given jobs as police. It was they who were given the assignment. At first, Sitting Bull seemed willing to go peacefully, but when he got out into the night air, surrounded by 40 policemen, he turned and announced that he wasn't going to go. Before the surprised police could act, one of the chief's close followers fired a shot and wounded one of them. As he fell he, in turn, shot Sitting Bull and

another policeman finished the job by firing a bullet into the old chief's head. Before the shooting stopped, six police and eight bystanders were killed.

Some months before, Sitting Bull had told his followers that a bird had told him that he would soon be killed by his own people.

The act threw the Indians into turmoil and put the Americans on alert. They deduced that another Sioux chief, Big Foot, would be the heir apparent to Sitting Bull, and the first order issued to the troops on that December day was to head south and put Big Foot under arrest. The chief and some 300 of his followers were rounded up and herded into a makeshift camp at Wounded Knee Creek in present-day South Dakota, just above the Nebraska border. The next step was to get the Indians to surrender their weapons. Sure they wouldn't give them up willingly, the American Colonel, James Forsyth, decided to take them by force. There were about 300 Indians, including women and children, facing nearly 500 soldiers. As the soldiers ransacked the Indian tipis looking for guns, the braves outside began to get restless. When the soldiers began to search them personally, one pulled a rifle from under his blanket and began firing. His shots were met with a volley from the Americans that cut down more than half the Indians. As the survivors began to charge, rapid-fire guns on all four sides opened up. One hundred thirty nine were killed instantly, the rest were wounded and left there to die. No attempt was made to go near the camp for three days because of an intense blizzard. When burial parties arrived on New Year's Day, 1891, they found four survivors, babies wrapped in blankets by their now dead mothers. The Indian wars were over.

Sitting Bull had been lured into his first season as a side show attraction by promoter Alvaren Allen, who promised the chief that his tour would take him through Washington, where he could present his case to the President of the United States. It never happened, and the following year he tossed another promoter out of his tipi for suggesting another tour. But the second promoter was better than the first, and what's more, he had an ace up his sleeve, a little girl named Annie Oakley. It was not for nothing that the man worked for the great Buffalo Bill. The showman knew that the only good thing that happened to Sitting Bull in his 1894 tour was meeting Annie Oakley, that he had named her "Little Miss Sure Shot" and had adopted her as his daughter. Annie worked for Buffalo Bill, too, and when he was told that, Sitting Bull signed a four-month contract. And though it wasn't promised in advance, he did get to meet President Grover Cleveland, for all the good it did.

Of all the characters produced by the Old West, few were more interesting than William F. Cody, who earned the name Buffalo Bill as a buffalo hunter supplying the men who were building the Kansas Pacific Railroad in 1868. In eight months working for the railroad he says he killed 4,280 of the beasts. But though he was one of the best of the hunters, he was much more than that. He had grown up on the Plains and had gone back and forth over the pioneer trails dozens of times, beginning when he was an 11-year-old employee of a wagon train. Over the years he was a miner, a trapper, a Pony Express rider. But his greatest moment came right after the Civil War when he acted as a scout for the U.S. Cavalry assigned to fight Indians on the Plains. It was said of him that he was involved in more fights with Indians than any scout of the period. It may have been true. He liked to fight, but fighting wasn't part of the job of a scout so the competition for the honor wasn't too tough.

Cody wasn't shy about telling stories of his exploits. He didn't even care if all the stories were true. But if people sometimes didn't believe him, he earned credibility after serving with General Philip Sheridan, who was very impressed by what he saw.

Buffalo Bill's stories were repeated to reporters from the East who considered him very good copy. Dime novels about him began appearing in the early 1870s and not long after that he accepted an offer to go on stage in Chicago as the star of a play about his exploits. But before he did, he wound up his days as a scout with a flourish.

When there were no troops to accompany, scouts were used to guide hunting parties through the wilderness. Wealthy Europeans, especially, flocked to the West to sample a type of hunting their less affluent neighbors could only imagine. They came with liveried servants who served them fine wine and French cuisine when they got back to camp at night. Cody didn't leave them lacking an image of the American frontiersman. He always wore a buckskin jacket and a brightly-colored shirt. He sat tall in the saddle on a fine horse, always white, and he wore a broad-brimmed hat, a Stetson, of course. There were many who said, and it may be true, that Buffalo Bill was in the pay of the Stetson Company and that he was the first cowboy figure to make a ten-gallon hat his trademark. While sipping champagne over a campfire, no one told better stories. And before long, Cody was in demand as a guide for all the best hunting parties.

The best of them all was in 1872 when the Grand Duke Alexis of Russia appeared in North Platte, Nebraska on a special train whose passenger list included General Sheridan, General Custer and Brigadier General Ord. The train also brought two companies of infantry, two of cavalry and a military band. But, except for the Grand

Duke himself, the man who stole the spotlight was William F. Cody, dressed for the occasion in fur-trimmed buckskin, his hair neatly curled and hanging just-so from under his famous broad-brimmed hat.

On the first day of the hunt, as was the custom, the Grand Duke downed the first buffalo with a lot of help from his experienced guide. To celebrate the occasion a bottle of champagne was produced, which prompted Cody to say later, "I was wishing he'd kill five or six more buffaloes before we reached camp, especially if a basket of champagne was to be produced every time he dropped one."

What entertainment he didn't provide in person, Cody had carefully arranged. Local Indians he had hired were on hand each evening to keep his guests occupied. And everything any of them did was carefully noted by the press corps that had been sent along to watch the famous Russian hunt. Buffalo Bill didn't know it for sure at that moment, but his days as a scout were numbered. He was about to yield to the lure of show business.

Bill went on the stage in Chicago in the winter of 1872. The play was called *The Scouts of the Prairie, or Red Deviltry As It Is.* It starred, as the advance publicity put it, "the real Buffalo Bill, Texas Jack and ten Sioux and Pawnee Chiefs." For men who liked their adventure in a slightly different form, the play also featured what a local reviewer identified as "a beautiful Indian maiden with an Italian accent and a weakness for scouts." The other Indians were fakes, too. Cody confessed in one of his autobiographies that the Sioux and Pawnee chiefs were otherwise out-of-work actors they found on the streets of Chicago.

The play had been written by Ned Buntline, who had a big hand in forming the Buffalo Bill legend as the author of dozens of dime novels about him. It had been reported that he wrote *The Scouts of the Prairie* in four hours, which prompted the critic from the *Tribune* to wonder what Ned had been doing all that time.

But though no one had anything good to say about it, it was historically significant for two reasons: it took Buffalo Bill off the prairie and into show business and it gave the world its first dramatic presentation of the Wild West. All those movies, all those TV shows full of blood and thunder owe their beginnings to what happened in Chicago in December, 1872, the night Princess Dove Eye, a.k.a. Giuseppina Morlacchi, walked onto the stage and seemed to fall head over heels in love with a golden-haired scout by the name of Buffalo Bill.

The audience loved him, too, and over the next ten years, in one-night stands all over the country, including in the Wild West itself, where they loved him most of all, Bill grew more famous and very rich.

But he grew restless, too. In the summer of 1882, in a Nebraska saloon not far from his ranch, he concocted an idea for a Fourth of July celebration. The more he drank, the more excited he got and the enthusiasm spread to the other patrons. It would be called the "Old Glory Blow Out" they decided. Some local businessmen offered to donate prizes for the best displays of bronco-riding, fancy shooting and horsemanship. Cody, who knew a little something about publicity, worked up a handbill explaining the whole thing, and a few days later he had more than a thousand eager participants. One local rancher donated a herd of buffalo so Bill could show them all how he went about killing so many so fast. The city fathers donated the fairgrounds, and before it was over, everyone for more than 200 miles around agreed it was the most glorious Fourth any of them had ever seen.

A half-century later, a Cody biographer said "...through Col. Cody's efforts and masterful personality, it became not only the progenitor of all the 'Frontier Day' state and inter-state tournaments...but to serve as the basic idea for an American revelation: border warfare and illustriously illustrative educational entertainment; the only one of its kind, and which has electrified and conquered the civilized world."

What Buffalo Bill invented for his Old Glory Blow Out, was more than a new way to celebrate a national holiday. He created the rodeo, for one thing, but more important for him, he had staged the world's first "Wild West" show.

He took Buffalo Bill's Wild West on the road in 1883. It was a show that included a herd of buffalo, which were lassoed and then ridden by some of the cowboys. The entourage consisted of cowboys and Indians (real this time), frontier scouts, and Mexican Vaqueros in glorious costume. The livestock ranged from mules and horses to mountain goats and a small elk herd. Bill bought the original Deadwood Stagecoach and reenacted an Indian attack on it as one of the highlights of the show. Fancy shooting was a great crowd-pleaser, too, as was bronco-riding. But Cody made it quite clear who was the star of the show, and the real highlights to watch for were the reenactments of his exploits as The Hero of The Plains.

The show reached its high-water mark in 1887 when Cody loaded his cowboys and Indians and all his livestock aboard a ship bound for England. He was already America's hero, but he hadn't seen anything yet.

When the Prince of Wales, the future King Edward VII, came to see the show, Cody wrote: "the Indians, yelling like fiends, galloped out and swept around the enclosure like a whirlwind. The effect was instantaneous and electric. The Prince rose from his seat, and the whole party seemed thrilled by the spectacle. 'Cody,' I said to myself, 'you have fetched 'em!'." He hadn't seen anything yet.

At that time, Queen Victoria had not been to a public entertainment in 25 years out of respect for her late husband, Prince Albert. It had become customary for entertainment to be brought to her in the privacy of Windsor Castle. But when she expressed a desire to see this Wild West show, it was pointed out that buffalo and elk and mountain sheep, not to mention wild Indians, would be out of place in the Royal residence. She agreed, and then also agreed that if the show couldn't come to her, she'd go to it.

Cody had made history again, but there was more to come. The show traditionally opened with a lusty ride around the arena in a salute to the American flag. At this performance, the Queen rose and bowed when the flag was presented. It was a gesture Cody was quick to take advantage of. In a press release dispatched back home, he said: "...There arose such a genuine heart-stirring American yell from our company as seemed to shake the sky. It was a great event. For the first time in history, since the Declaration of Independence, a sovereign of Great Britain had saluted the star-spangled banner, and that banner was carried by a member of Buffalo Bill's Wild West!"

During their stay in England, the attack on the Deadwood Stage, the reenactments of Custer's Last Stand, the burning of a settler's cabin by evil Red Men, the hardships of a wagon Train and Buffalo Bill's exploits as an Indian fighter were seen by the kings of Greece, Denmark, Saxony and Belgium. Queen Kapiolani of

Hawaii, The Queen of the Belgians and a man who claimed the throne of France all saw the show. It enthralled princes and princesses, too, including the Crown Princes of Germany, Austria, Sweden and Norway, Portugal, Siam and Bavaria.

The tour that followed put the American West on the map as far as Europe was concerned, and started a love affair that hasn't stopped yet.

Cody assembled an aggregation of people often as famous as himself. In addition to Annie Oakley and Sitting Bull, he hired men like Pawnee Bill and Buck Taylor, the first ever to be known as "King of the Cowboys." He had appeared on stage with his old friend Wild Bill Hickok, whose career as an actor was short-lived because it was said "he had a voice like a girl." But if a man wasn't famous in his own right, Bill didn't care. He hired the sheriff of his adopted home town in Nebraska, a fellow named Cor Croner, and billed him as the man who has captured "over fifty murderers and more than that number of horse thieves, cattle rustlers, burglars and outlaws." Cody also credited Croner with thwarting an attempted train robbery by "followers" of Jesse James. But then, Jesse James had a lot of followers, if not confederates.

Jesse and his brother Frank, along with their partners Cole and Jim Younger was said to have begun their careers as desperadoes in Liberty, Missouri, in 1866 where they held up a bank and rode off with $75,000. By 1870, they were wanted in two states, Missouri and Kentucky, for bank robbery. And after April 27, 1872, when they killed a bank cashier, they were wanted for murder. A year later, they moved through Iowa and then, in front of 20,000 witnesses, they held up the Kansas City Fair and casually took the entire day's receipts.

Every time they robbed a bank, which was often, their reputation increased. And after every bank robbery, the size of the posse that took off after them got bigger, too. After a job in Missouri, the gang left a trail of paper for the posse to follow. Written on each piece was the message: "Married men turn around and go home. Single men follow." The boys didn't want to be responsible for creating any widows and orphans, even if they didn't mind taking their savings from the local banks.

The James gang was famous all over the country by 1873 as the most daring bank robbers the West had produced. But they had a new career in mind by then. In the middle of the night of July 20, 1873, the locomotive of a Chicago, Rock Island and Pacific train turned over when it hit a rail that had been pried loose near Council Bluffs, Iowa. The sobotage was the work of the James boys, who then took everything of any value from the baggage car. Before they rode off, they wandered through the train and took money, watches and other jewelry from the terrified passengers. It was the first time anyone had ever thought of holding up a train.

The posse never caught up with the bandits, but the bandits caught up with another train about six months later. This time, they took control of an out-of-the-way railroad station and put out a "stop" signal for the next passenger train through. When the train obeyed the signal, they boarded it, robbed the passengers and looted the baggage car. Before they left, one of the outlaws gave the conductor an envelope which he said he wanted delivered to the local newspaper. "This is the exact story of how we did this holdup," he explained, "we're tired of the papers getting the stories all wrong." The papers nearly got a better story. The posse tracked the outlaws to a cave in the Missouri hills. The trail led in, but not out, so a guard was set. But by the time they thought they had enough reinforcements to beard the lions in their den, the gang had already escaped by swimming an underground river.

Oddly, though they had a string of killings to their credit and had been instrumental in making travel by train or stagecoach or even visiting a bank a risky business in a half-dozen states, the James boys enjoyed more public admiration than they probably deserved. Their flamboyance was part of it; they had the law running in circles. But probably more important was that all the members of the James gang were veterans of the Confederate Army. In the mid-19th century, thousands from the defeated South went west to find new lives. The Establishment there was largely made up of people with sympathies to the Union cause. Outlaws like Jesse James did what all the newcomers wanted to do: give the Yankees a hard time and get rich in the process. But no matter what, Jesse was still an outlaw, and if posses couldn't catch him, the Establishment reasoned, it was time to hire someone who could.

The someone was the great private detective Allan Pinkerton. He didn't come himself at first, but sent one of his ace operatives who turned up dead one morning, another of Jesse James's victims. That goaded Pinkerton into going to Missouri himself. His plan was to surround the home of Jesse's mother and stepfather, where it was well-known the gang was hiding out, and to force them to come out with a bomb if he had to. But Jesse had a lot of friends in Missouri and before the Pinkerton gang arrived at the farmhouse, the James gang was miles away. But Pinkerton didn't know that and in frustration, he tossed his bomb. It killed Jesse's halfbrother and tore off his mother's arm. It also gave Jesse James more public sympathy than he'd ever had before. A bill was introduced in the Missouri Legislature to give the gang amnesty. "Driven as they are from the fields of honest industry, from their friends and from this home," said the proposed legislation, "...they can feel no allegiance to a government which forces them to the very acts it professes to deprecate, and then offers a bounty for their apprehension, and arms foreign mercenaries with power to capture and kill them." In language only a lawyer could love, the bill went on to say that the boys probably didn't do all those bad things anyway and it was time that the real perpetrators, "those pretending to hunt them," were exposed for the rascals they are.

The bill never passed and the Jameses stayed away from their friends and their home. But outside their home territory, nobody knew what they looked like, and they led a fairly good life spending their money in Eastern cities. Both got married, both had children, neither raised families in the territories where they "worked."

The James boys never had much problem recruiting members for their gang. The pay was good and the risk was small. But their luck began to change in 1876 when they took on a bank in Northfield, Minnesota. A local businessmen saw what was going on inside the bank and rounded up armed citizens who were waiting for the robbers when they came out. In the shooting that followed, several bystanders were killed, but so were two of the bandits. And the gang was forced to retreat without any of their loot. Nothing like that had ever happened to the James boys in a whole decade of shooting up small towns. And then something worse happened: the inevitable posse caught up with them. In the fight that followed, one gang member was killed and Bob, Cole and Jim Younger were severely wounded. Cole took 11 bullets, his brother, Jim, stopped five. All three wound up with life sentences in a Minnesota Penitentiary, hardly a predictable fate for three of the most famous desperadoes of the Wild West.

Jesse and Frank escaped and headed south through Nebraska and Texas until they were safely south of the border in Mexico. They came back time after time, according to most accounts, stopping an occasional train or relieving stage passengers of their rings and watches. Jesse finally moved with his wife and children to a house in St. Joseph, Missouri. What he didn't know was that the Kansas City police had hired one of his gang members, Bob Howard, to kill him. The deed was done, with a bullet to the head fired from a gun Jesse himself had given Howard the day before. The whole country was outraged that an "innocent" man should be shot down by a killer hired by the police. The outrage lasted for years and because of it, when Frank was arrested and tried for his crimes, he was acquitted because of what had happened to his brother.

It all seems so long ago. Yet as recently as the mid-1950s, a man, an old man, to be sure, told the world that Howad had killed the wrong man and that he was the real Jesse James. And people believed him. There are people alive today whose grandparents thrilled to the exploits of Annie Oakley and Buffalo Bill and probably saw Sitting Bull in person. But though Lewis and Clark took the civilized world west for the first time less than 200 years ago, neither of them would recognize much of the territory if they were to explore it today. An Interstate highway follows much of the old Oregon Trail. The great waterfall where the Missouri River came out of the mountains, once so spectacular it could be heard for miles, has been eliminated by a series of dams. But for all that, the countryside is still wildly beautiful, still untamed in many places as far as the eye can see.

The bison don't roam the Plains any longer, most of the gold that lured so many to go so far is buried in Eastern vaults. The railroads, built with such incredible labor, that made getting there a little more fun and provided a dandy source of income for the likes of Jesse James, still exist, but not so many are as eager to buy passenger tickets as they were in Jesse's day.

But the spirit of the West is alive and well. Today's cowboy is as likely to work his herd in a pickup truck or a helicopter as with a pony. And not everyone who wears a ten-gallon hat and enjoys resting his boots on the brass rail at the local saloon is likely to be a real cowpuncher, except on weekends.

Though you'd be hard-pressed these days to find a grizzled old prospector leading a loaded mule over a mountain pass, it isn't at all unusual to see people hiking with little picks and shovels. Chances are good they're not geologists, but local folks operating on hope. Hope is part of the Western tradition. It was what brought many to the West in the first place and, along with faith, what kept them going once they got there. Winning it wasn't easy. But it was worth the effort.

Hardly anyone seeing the American West for the first time can avoid the feeling of spaciousness. There's room to stretch your spirits in mountains more beautiful than any others on earth, in deserts so vast, canyons so deep, rivers and streams so clear. The air is uncommonly clear in most of the West, too. And at night there are more stars in the sky than people in lesser places get to see in all the nights of a lifetime put together.

There are problems of pollution, too, and urban sprawl. There is thoughtless litter, often in unlikely places. And taco stands, used car lots, hamburger dispensaries and motels. But there are rainbows, too, and a recurring dream that this is where you can find your pot of gold in the form of a better life.

Mark Twain went west in a stagecoach in the 1850s, looking for adventure rather than riches. The adventure paid off in the form of a book called "Roughing It," which helped explain why he didn't settle down and become a writer of Western yarns. His destination was Carson City, Nevada. "It was a 'wooden town,' its population about two thousand souls," he wrote. "The main street consisted of four or five blocks of little white frame stores...packed close together side by side as if room were scarce in that mighty plain. The sidewalk was of boards that were more or less loose and inclined to rattle when walked upon. In the middle of the town, opposite the stores, was the 'plaza' which is native to all the towns west of the Rocky Mountains – a large unfenced vacancy with a liberty pole in it, and very useful as a place for public auctions, horse trades and mass meetings, and likewise for teamsters to camp in. Two other sides of the plaza were faced by stores, offices and stables. The rest of Carson City was pretty scattering."

He wasn't impressed by the towns he visited, and, in fact, didn't stay long. But he did fall in love with the West in the same way people do today. He said:

"If there is any life that is happier than the life we led (during) the next two or three weeks, it must be the sort of life which I have not read of in books or experienced in person. We did not see a human being but ourselves during the time, or hear any sounds but those that were made by the wind and the waves, the sighing of the pines and, now and then, the far-off thunder of an avalanche. The forest about us was dense and cool, and sky above was cloudless and brilliant with sunshine, the broad lake before us was glassy and clear, or rippled and breezy, or black and storm-tossed, according to Nature's mood; and its circling border of mountain domes, clothed with forests, scarred with landslides, cloven by canyons and valleys and helmeted with

glittering snow, fitly framed and finished the noble picture. The view was always fascinating, bewitching, entrancing. The eye never tired of gazing, night or day, in calm or in storm; it suffered but one grief, and that was that it could not look always, but must close sometimes in sleep.

"...While smoking the pipe of peace after breakfast we watched the sentinel peaks put on the glory of the sun, and followed the conquering light as it swept down among the shadows and set the captive crags and forests free. We watched the tinted pictures grow and brighten upon the water till every little detail of forest, precipice and pinnacle was wrought in and finished, and the miracle of the enchanter complete.

"Then to 'business.' That is, drifting around in the boat...So singularly clear was the water, that where it was only twenty or thirty feet deep the bottom was so perfectly distinct that the boat seemed floating in the air! Yes, where it was *eighty* feet deep, every little pebble was distinct, every speckled trout, every hand's-breadth of sand. ...So empty and airy did all the spaces seem below us, so strong the sense of floating high aloft in mid-nothingness, that we called these boat excursions 'balloon voyages'."

The identical experience is possible right now in many parts of the West.

But if Mark Twain was impressed by the spectacle nature provides in the American West, the people he met were something else again:

"A young half-breed with a complexion like a yellow-jacket asked me if I would have my boots blacked. I said yes, and he blacked them. Then I handed him a silver five-cent piece with a benevolent air of a person who is conferring wealth and blessedness upon poverty and suffering. The yellow-jacket took it with what I judged to be suppressed emotion, and laid it reverently down in the middle of his broad hand. Then he began to contemplate it, much as a philosopher contemplates a gnat's ear in the ample field of his microscope. Several mountaineers, teamsters, stage-drivers, etc, drew near and dropped into the tableau and fell to surveying the money with that attractive indifference to formality with is noticeable in the hardy pioneer.

"Presently the yellow-jacket handed the half-dime back to me and told me I ought to keep my money in my pocket-book instead of in my soul, then I wouldn't get it cramped and shriveled up so!

"Yes, we had learned...to be charged great prices without letting the inward shudder appear on the surface, for we had already overheard and noted the tenor of conversations until we were well aware that these superior beings despised 'emigrants.' We permitted no tell-tale shudders and winces in our countenances, for we wanted to seem pioneers, or Mormons, half-breeds, teamsters, stage-drivers, mountain meadow assassins – anything in the world that the plains respected and admired – but we were wretchedly ashamed of being 'emigrants' and sorry that we had white shirts and could not swear in the presence of ladies without looking the other way."

If the rough edges of the landscape are still there, most of the rough edges in the people have vanished since the 1850s, and today's Westerner is generally warm and friendly and likes few things more than showing off this wonderful land. And most of them, even if their grandparents were born there and they've never bothered to cross the Mississippi or even wonder what's on the other side, they still refer to anything between St. Louis and the Atlantic Ocean as "back East." And most of them sincerely believe that anyone who chooses to live "back East" is surely more to be pitied than censured.

In front of the Alamo is the War Memorial *right* which commemorates the heroic struggle for Texan independence. In the view *facing page* from the top of the Tower of the Americas, the main features of central San Antonio can be clearly seen. The tower stands in the HemisFair Plaza, as do the sculptures *below and far right*. The plaza is a legacy of the great world fair of 1968. *Overleaf, left* the Melodrama Theater in HemisFair Plaza, just south of the legendary Alamo *overleaf, right*.

San Antonio: *top left and top right* **Downtown dancers,** *above* **Alamo Place,** *right* **Texas Institute of Culture.** *Facing page: top right* **a memorial on the River Walk** *top left,* **Botanical Gardens** *bottom right* **and** *bottom left and top center* **Alamo Grounds.** *Overleaf* **scenes along the River Walk.**

AN OLD LEGEND
DESCRIBES THIS
TWIN CYPRESS AS
A LOOKOUT OF A
MEXICAN SNIPER
WHO PICKED OFF THE
TEXANS AS THEY
CAME TO THE
RIVER FOR
WATER

In 1839, President Mirabeau Lamar of Texas sent out five horsemen to find a site for the national capital. They returned having found a spot on the Colorado River. The new city was named after Stephen Austin, the "Father of Texas." The beautiful, pink granite capitol *above and facing page* is the largest state capitol in America. In the capitol grounds stand several statues, including a monument to the Terry Rangers *above*. Town Lake *right* is part of an extensive water system. The Lyndon B. Johnson Library *top right* is one of the finest in the country.

The Reunion Tower *left and overleaf, left* houses a revolving restaurant and cocktail bar, which give magnificent views across Dallas. Behind the tower stands the modern Hyatt Regency Hotel. *Above* Ervay St. and *facing page* Old City Park. *Overleaf, right* Municipal Plaza Park.

The Texas State Fair Park *these pages* stands just outside Dallas. It was constructed in the 1930s as a home for the Dallas museums.

Its imposing buildings and monuments are the setting for the State Fair of Texas. The Fair lasts for sixteen exciting days in October every year.

Previous pages: *righthand page, right* the Reunion Tower, *left* Thanks-Giving Square; *lefthand page, bottom left* the Hyatt Regency Hotel, *top center* Municipal Plaza Park, *bottom center* the Mobil Building. *This page*

Old City Park has some 25 restored or rebuilt buildings in their pioneer state. *Facing page* Reunion Tower. *Overleaf, left: top left* Municipal Plaza, *bottom left* Thanks-Giving Square, *bottom right* Hyatt Regency Hotel.

Previous page: bottom left **the Classical architecture of the Texas State Fair Park,** *top center* **the elegant war memorial before the Convention Center,** *top right and bottom center* **Municipal Plaza. Fort Worth** *these pages* **has grown rapidly in recent decades.**

Corpus Christi stands about halfway along the Texas Coast and, with a population pushing a quarter of a million, is an important port and industrial center. But it is far better known as a tourist and convention resort. Its sandy beaches, fine hotels and above all the marina *these pages* draw people from right across the Lone Star State.

The city of Galveston *these and previous pages* stands on Galveston Island, two miles offshore. Its beautiful climate and thirty-two-mile beach have made Galveston a popular resort, the tourists staying in such hotels as the Flagship *far left* and the Galvez *previous page.* Shops *below left* offer souvenirs along the seawall. *Below* the Sacred Heart School and Church. Ashton Villa *facing page* was built in 1859 and has withstood both the ravages of the Civil War and the hurricane of 1900 to become the city's oldest house open to the public.

Galveston Island *these pages* was discovered in 1686 by the intrepid Frenchman La Salle and named St. Louis, but it did not gain its present name until the Spanish arrived in 1777 and called it Galvez. The shallow waters of the island have many piers including that *above* at Stewart Beach and *facing page* at Galveston sea front.

Galveston has a fine harbor *top left and facing page* and surfing beaches *above*. *Top right* the pier off Galveston sea front. Seawolf Park *right*, with its warships, playgrounds and picnic areas, is one of the city's greatest attractions.

Extending some 750 miles in length and breadth, the huge Texas landscape displays a magnificent variety of scenery, seen in Pulliam Ridge, at the edge of the Chisos Basin *facing page,* **and the Rio Grande as it flows into the waters of Lake Amistad** *above.*

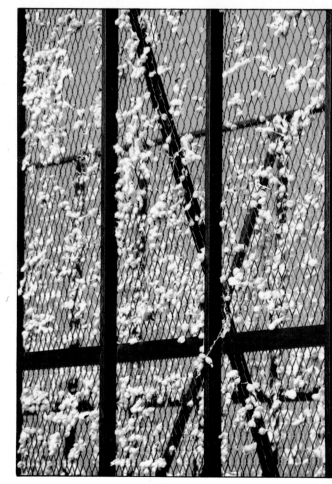

Texas cattle are still traded at Amarillo *far left* and *top right*, but cotton *left* remains important. The modern architecture of El Paso's Civic Center *facing page* contrasts with the older style of the Alamo *above*. *Top left* Cadillac Ranch.

Big Bend National Park is nestled in the arid, rugged and forbidding great curve of the Rio Grande, in Southwest Texas. *Above:* **the Park's Christmas Mountains.** *Facing page:* **the size of the figure in the canoe gives some idea of the immensity of Santa Elena Canyon in Big Bend.**

Taos is a picturesque New Mexico city. In the nearby Pueblo *facing page* is the graceful church *left*. The Mission of San Miguel *bottom left* in Santa Fe is one of the oldest churches in the country. *Below* the ruins of Fort Union National Monument. *Bottom right* Tucson Civic Center.

Silhouetted by the late evening sun, a lone tree *above* **in New Mexico's Gila National Forest.** *Facing page:* **the sun breaks through the clouds above the Sangre de Cristo Mountains, New Mexico.**

Among the commoner plants in the Guadaloupe National Park is the spiky, smooth-leafed sotol *facing page*, pictured with Hunter Peak in the background. *Above:* Inscription Rock at El Morro National Monument, New Mexico.

Formed in a limestone reef by percolating ground water, the vast underground chambers of the Carlsbad Caverns *above and facing page* are situated beneath the rugged foothills of New Mexico's Guadaloupe Mountains. In this subterranean wonderland the huge galleries are filled with delicate stone formations, massive stalactites and stalagmites which, colored by the minerals and iron they contain, produce a fascinating, iridescent glow.

The Saguaro National Monument *facing page* **contains dense stands of Saguaro cactus which can live up to 200 years, reaching heights of 36 feet and, exceptionally, 50 feet. Aloof and gaunt, the massive bulk of Shiprock** *below* **is seen sharply outlined against a glowing sunset.**

Canyon de Chelly *left* **in Arizona, contains evidence of five different periods of Indian culture.** *Above:* **Little Colorado River Gorge, near Gray Mountain.**

Different moods *above and left,* **but equally awe-inspiring:
East and West Mittens, with Merrick Butte, in Monument
Valley's Navajo Trail Park.**

Arizona's scenery and monuments rank among the most magnificent in the country. Oak Creek Canyon is shown *above* while *facing page* is pictured majestic Monument Valley.

Arizona's Petrified Forest is unique among the
petrifications of the world in its size, variety and scope.
Facing page: logs turned to stone over the ages lie scattered
in Blue Mesa. *Above:* Painted Desert – a strange landscape
of weird shapes and marvelous variety of color.

**Wherever the eye rests there is something new to be seen
of the ancient and incredible landscapes of the Grand
Canyon** *facing page* **and the Petrified Forest National Park**
above.

From the majestic peaks of Hopi Point *above and facing page* **the splendor of the Grand Canyon's South Rim fans out to meet the horizon.**

The Grand Canyon has often been described as a sight too staggering, too vast for the imagination to take in. *Facing page:* the view from Moran Point and *above* from Yaki Point.

At times, depending on the light and the weather, the
Grand Canyon can appear forbidding, frightening almost;
at other times, as here in the views from Mohave Point
above and Yaki Point *facing page,* there is an aura of peace;
a mystic stillness.

In Grand Canyon, layer upon layer of stratified rock rises
from the canyon floor, where the Colorado River, seen at
Lee's Ferry *above,* winds like a slender ribbon. Reflecting
the sun's warm rays stands the brilliantly-colored rock
formation of Cathedral Rock *facing page* at Red Rock
Crossing in Sedona's Oak Creek Canyon.

In the Glen Canyon National Recreation Area is Glen Canyon Dam *left. Below* St. Mary's Church, Phoenix, and the sculpture of the *Phoenix Bird Ascending. Bottom left* the White House, Canyon de Chelly National Monument. *Bottom right* Tombstone, the "Town too tough to die". *Facing page* Old Tuscon, erected in 1940 as a film location by Columbia Pictures.

The Hoover Dam *facing page*, at 726 feet, is one of
the highest dams ever constructed. *Above* a giant
Saguaro cactus in Desert Foothills, Phoenix,
Arizona.

Brooding in the distance, Superstition Mountains *above* **take their name from the legends handed down in which they feature. Fields of alfalfa** *facing page* **are watered by the essential irrigation system provided by a series of dams throughout Arizona.**

Denver, the 'Mile High City' and capital of Colorado, is an important financial and trading center. Spread over some 100 square miles, the city boasts a modern and impressive Downtown skyline *facing page* comprising soaring skyscrapers and thoughtfully preserved old buildings. Pictured *above* is the magnificent gold-domed Capitol building seen across the landscaped grounds of the Civic Center.

**Each season has its own especial beauty, but the magic of
fall has, for most people, an irresistible charm, as here in
Colorado's Crystal Creek** *above* **and Independence Pass**
facing page.

Horses grazing *above* **against the backdrop of a Colorado forest.** *Facing page:* **Dream Lake with Hallett Peak and Flattop Mountain in the background.**

Overleaf, left the tranquil scene at Beaver Ponds, in Hidden Valley, Colorado. *Overleaf, right* Maroon Creek snakes its way towards Aspen before meeting the rush of the Roaring Fork River.

The textured timbers of a long-discarded wagon *facing page*
echo the desolation of the town of Ashcroft. The scattered
remains of this once-busy township are now preserved by the
Aspen Historical Society. *Above* perched on a rocky outcrop
by the Crystal River lie the remains of Deadhorse Mill.

Typical of the 1860s character of Black Hawk is the ornate Lace House, with its carved gingerboard trimming *bottom* and the white weatherboarded building *below*. The town's brightly painted Crook's Palace lays claim to the title – "Oldest Bar in Colorado." Historic Central City *facing page,* scene of frenetic activity during the height of the gold rush, is now a sleepy town of some 300 inhabitants. *Bottom left:* Boodle Mine near Central City.

Carved by the incessant flow of the meandering Green River *this page*, the spectacular Lodore Canyon rises to a height of 3,300 feet. *Facing page:* a panoramic view of canyon country and Round Top Mountain.

**The lofty peaks of the magnificent Sawatch Range, which
includes some of Colorado's highest mountains, drop
steeply to the lapping waters of the Twin Lakes on
Independence Pass** *above and facing page.*

Seen from a distance across the sprawling, scrub-covered
San Luis Valley, even the mighty mountains appear
intimidated by the oppressive, leaden sky *above*. Huddled
together as if for protection, the forests of aspen *facing
page* spread their warm colors over the land.

A cluster of wooden houses nestled high in the San Juan Mountains of southwestern Colorado make up the small community of Telluride. Originally a bustling town named for the element tellurium found in the ores of the region, Telluride's older buildings *below and left* serve as reminders of its colorful past. Today, the town is undergoing another boom with the development of skiing facilities. Silvertown, with its preserved buildings *bottom left* and narrow gauge railway *bottom right,* was once the center of the San Juan mining industry. *Facing page:* the 'Sunshine City' of Colorado Springs, with the Broadmoor Hotel complex center left of picture.

Home for innumerable species of birds and animal life, **Rocky Mountain National Park** *right, far right and bottom right* **is an impressive mixture of fish-filled lakes, breathtaking mountain scenery and deep wooded valleys. Its 410 square miles of natural beauty are a major tourist attraction throughout the year, offering facilities for the skier, climber, fisherman and horserider.** *Below:* **hardy conifers carpet the lower slopes of the Snaffels Range in southwestern Colorado.** *Facing page:* **dotted with countless mountain peaks, Gunnison National Forest lies at the western edge of the Rockies.**

Estes Park, cradled in a valley at the eastern edge of the Rocky Mountain National Park, is a popular winter and summer holiday resort which, with the attractions of its surrounding wilderness, offers the visitor an unparalleled range of outdoor activities. Approached from the south by the impressive Million Dollar Highway, the scenic town of Ouray *facing page* **is encircled by the 14,000 foot high peaks of the Uncompahgre National Forest.**

Like an extension of the natural rock that cocoons it, the 'Square Tower House' *above*, in Mesa Verde's Navajo Canyon, blends with its austere surroundings. Equally awe-inspiring are the strangely contorted rock formations of Monument Canyon shown *facing page* with the Book Cliff Mountains in the distance.

Steep sided mountains dotted with old mine workings,
form a natural pocket for the town of Ouray *these pages.*
Named after the peacemaking chieftain of the Southern
Utes, Ouray stands on ground that was considered sacred
by the Indians. One of the popular attractions in Ouray
itself is the outdoor swimming pool fed by the warm
geothermal springs.

Against the huge ball of the setting sun, trucks *above* cross
a bridge near Las Cruces, Colorado, and *facing page* an
electric storm demonstrates its power above the state's
Mesa Verde National Park.

As if magically transported from some coastal location, the shifting shapes of the Great Sand Dunes National Monument extend for ten miles beneath the looming bulk of the Sangre de Cristo Range's western slopes *facing page.* Equally unusual are the bright sandstone structures to be found in the Garden of the Gods near Colorado Springs *above.*

Overleaf, left **Cliff Palace is probably the most famous of all the Pueblo cliff dwellings to be found in Mesa Verde National Park** *overleaf, right.*

Steamboat Springs *these pages,* so called because of the hot mineral springs to be found in the area, is one of the many Colorado winter resorts which offer the visitor a wide variety of seasonal activities. In addition to the superb slopes that cater for skiers of all standards, visitors can enjoy the popular sleigh rides, ski-jumping and skating, as well as the relaxation of swimming in the hot spring pools.

Above: **the soaring beauty of majestic Double Arch, in Utah's Arches National Park.** *Facing Page:* **Bryce Canyon, Southern Utah.**

In Canyonlands National Park, Utah, the sun silhouettes both tiny figures and massive rock formations *above*, seen from Big Spring Canyon Overlook. Arches National Park lies in the famous red rock country of Utah and contains more natural stone arches – such as Delicate Arch *facing page* – windows, spires and pinnacles than anywhere else in the country.

The colorful and quite incredible formations in Bryce
Canyon are the result of rocks, shale and sandstones which
have all eroded at different rates, allowing the elements to
create fantastic sculptures and free-standing columns
above. The last of the sun just catches one of the peaks at
Paria View *facing page*.

Heavy clouds gathering at Bryce Canyon's Paria View *above.* **One of the remarkable scenes** *facing page* **on the Fairyland Trail, Bryce Canyon, Utah.**

Left: **Bryce Point, Bryce Canyon National Park.** *Above:* **an ink-black sky adds drama – if that were possible – to the pinnacles, spires and slopes seen from Inspiration Point.**

Zion Canyon, in Zion National Park, Utah, is a spectacular multicolored gorge, where gigantic stone masses such as the Watchman *left* **and the Sentinel** *above,* **may be seen across the waters of the North Fork of the Virgin River.**

Lower Green Lake and Flattop Mountain *above*. **Burnished at sunset, Wyoming's Jackson Lake** *facing page* **is a natural lake formed in a deep groove left by a piedmont glacier which passed through Jackson Hole during the first Ice Age.**

Minerva Terrace *above,* **Mammoth Hot Springs,
Yellowstone National Park, is composed of travertine, a
form of calcium carbonate that has been dissolved from
limestone beneath the ground and carried to the surface by
hot water.** *Facing page:* **thick snow covers the ground as it
spreads towards the Grand Tetons.**

Bison *facing page* **at the aptly-named Opalescent Pool,
which brings ever changing shades to Black Sand Basin.**
Above: **Yellowstone's Morning Glory Pool, complete with
name plaque.**

The Lower Falls *above* **crash down over 300 feet into the
yawning, mist-laden Grand Canyon of the Yellowstone River.
Rather more modest and graceful are the Upper Falls** *facing
page*, **which arch down for over 100 feet.**

Fire-Ball River, colored as befits its name *facing page*, curves through Wyoming's Midway Geyser. Part of the natural beauty which makes Yellowstone so idyllic a preserve, the Gibbon River *below* threads its silver waters between the trees and grassland of its banks.

Producing clouds of steam, even in winter, Midway Geyser
Basin, Wyoming, is pictured *above*. The peaks of the Grand
Teton Range rise beyond the waters of the Snake River at
Oxbow Bend *facing page.*

Sculpted by glaciers during the Ice Age, the serrated peaks of the Grand Tetons, form a magnificent backdrop for the autumnal-hued trees *above* **as they rise abruptly from the valley floor.** *Facing page* **the Morning Glory Pool, Yellowstone National Park, Wyoming.**

Overleaf, left **the spirit of the Wild West lives on in the shape of a stagecoach.** *Overleaf, right* **bison graze during a dull winter's day at Black Sand Basin.**

The Badlands National Monument *these pages* **lies in
southwestern South Dakota. It was established in 1939 in
the area between the Cheyenne and White Rivers. The
monument contains numerous fossil beds in which has been
found evidence of such exotic animals as the sabre-toothed
tiger and the rhinoceros.**

These pages depicting the faces of four presidents, Mount Rushmoor National Memorial, North Dakota, towers majestically over the pine-covered Black Hills.

Bison *above*, **remnants of the huge herds that once roamed the prairies, at peace in Badlands National Park, South Dakota.** *Facing page* **a heavily clouded sky above flooded grasslands in Montana.**

The Wild West lives again in the scenes *above and facing page* **during Monterey's annual bison round-up.**

Sunrise goldens Mount Sinopah, beyond the shores of Two Medicine Lake *above* **and jagged mountains surround St. Mary Lake and Wild Geese Island** *facing page*, **in Glacier National Park, Montana.**

These pages **Boise, capital of Idaho.** *Top left* **Old St. Michael's Church.** *Top right and right* **State Capitol Building.** *Facing page* **Union Station with a nearby sign** *above.*

Above **view of Boise from Union Station.** *Facing page* **the
city at night.** *Overleaf* **views of the city dominated by
mountains. Boise was named by French-Canadian trappers of
the early 19th century because of its tree-lined river,
the French word** *boisé* **meaning wooded.**

Reno *facing page* **and Las Vegas** *this page*, Nevada's fun-loving cities, glitter and sparkle twenty-four hours a day with a wealth of gambling casinos and fabulous entertainments – *left* the Folies-Bergère at the Tropicana Hotel, Las Vegas – that draw millions of visitors annually to these internationally-famous resorts.

Above the gold-rush town of Virginia City, Nevada. *Facing page* the buildings of Bodie are now part of a State Historic Park. Once it was a booming gold-mining town with a far-flung notoriety. At its peak, this "den of iniquity" supported 65 saloons and there was an average of one murder a day.

These pages: **golden California, land of sunshine, mists and rolling hills. It is also a land of rich diversity.** *Left* **Sherman Gilbert House, San Diego Old Town, with similarly styled buildings** *below.* **Balboa Park** *bottom left* **and the Coronado Hotel** *bottom right. Facing page:* **San Diego harbor.**

This page: left **the Charthouse Golf Course and the graceful sweep of the San Diego-Coronado Bay Bridge.** *Below left* **many of the old adobe buildings in the Old Town have been converted from their original use as part of Mission San Diego de Alcala, into quaint restaurants and shops.** *Below* **standing serenely in the Californian sunshine, Mission San Diego was founded by Padre Juniper Serra and is known as the "Mother of Missions".**

Facing page: left **La Jolla, north of San Diego, enjoys all the benefits of sun, sand and sea. Here is also the Scripps Institution of Oceanography and the Salk Institute for Biological Studies. Just off the coast lies an extensively studied submarine canyon, known as Scripps Canyon.** *Top right* **the California Tower in Balboa Park.** *Center right* **the fine and historic Hotel Del Coronado.** *Bottom right* **the old lighthouse was erected on top of Point Loma in 1855. However, because its light was often obscured by cloud, the present Coast Guard Lighthouse was built, in 1891, close to the water's edge.**

Facing page: left the winding magnificence of the stairway at Mission Inn. The building is rightly recognized as one of the most beautiful in California, although its origins were as a humble adobe cottage begun in 1875. *Top right* the fourth mission to be dedicated in California was Mission San Gabriel with its cool, vaulted cloisters. *Bottom right* Santa Barbara Court House resembles a Spanish-Moorish castle.

This page: top left the cool, landscaped features of the Walter Annenberg Estate, Palm Springs. *Left and above* the J. Paul Getty Museum has been set out in the style of the Villa dei Papiri, which was sited in the ancient city of Herculaneum, near Pompeii, around the 1st century. The Museum building contains marble and bronze sculptures, mosaics and vases, with a wide selection of Western pictorial art.

Below **Bonaventure Hotel.** *Left* **wonderful, wealthy Beverly Hills with its lush Plaza.** *Facing page* **the palatial Hotel Beverly Wilshire. The 207-acre Huntingdon estate** *bottom right* **contains a well-planned Botanical Gardens and the Library and Art Gallery building. The Court House in Santa Barbara** *bottom left* **reflects images of "Old Spain".**

Los Angeles *previous pages* takes on an oriental aspect in its Chinatown *these pages*, where the images suggested by the pagoda-style buildings are compounded by the pungence of aromatic spices and incense. Here you can indulge yourself with delicious Chinese cuisine or just meander through the bustling streets. Sited on Hollywood Boulevard is Mann's Chinese Theater *facing page, bottom right*, where the footprints, handprints and signatures of the movie stars are immortalized in concrete.

Los Angeles displays many fine new buildings in its city center. *Left* the Union Bank Building and the Bonaventure Hotel. The magnificent Dorothy Chandler Pavilion *below* and the Mark Taper Forum *bottom left*, together with the Ahmanson Theater, form the Los Angeles Music Center for the Performing Arts. *Bottom right* the Century Plaza and Schubert Theater. Traffic flows along the Harbor Freeway *facing page* in the Downtown area.

In the Botanical Gardens at Huntington *left* there is an immense variety of cacti and other flora to be seen. *Below* California's favorable climate ensures the presence of the ubiquitous palm trees *below* lining the streets. *Bottom* situated in San Pedro, along the main channel of Los Angeles Harbor, Ports O'Call and Whaler's Wharf recapture the atmosphere of New England seacoast villages. Colonial style shops and restaurants, with their quaint, tavern-like signs outside, line the cobbled streets.

Facing page: Pasadena is well known for its Rose Bowl Stadium where, on New Year's Day, football fans fill the arena to watch this classic championship match. *Top left* the City Hall, in all its ornate glory, reflects the Spanish inspired architecture which was popular in the 1920s. *Remaining photographs* Los Angeles is justly famous for its racing parks, such as Santa Anita Park and Hollywood Park Racetrack, many containing magnificent tropical gardens and elegant restaurants as well as some of the world's top racehorses on the flat, or trotting *bottom right* in lightweight two-wheeled sulkies.

This page: **harbor fishing boats, yachts and tuna clippers crowd Ports O'Call and Whaler's Wharf.** *Above and right* **ever-popular skateboarding. Los Angeles, sunny pleasure land of the West, is full of possibilities for the young at heart. Newport Beach and Balboa is 35 miles south of Los Angeles, attracting fishermen** *facing page, bottom right* **to its shores.**

Universal City Studios *this page* is the largest motion-picture studio in the world. Two and a half million visitors come to Universal each year and conducted tours are provided. There are many different sets to be seen, from the Wild West, where stuntmen show their skills *above and top right*, to the ferocious shark *right* from *Jaws*. *Facing page:* after 31 years of Atlantic crossings, the *Queen Mary* now rests at Long Beach. The stately liner's attractions include shops, restaurants and a marine exhibition.

Disneyland is Walt Disney's "Magic Kingdom" *these pages*. Built on 150 acres, it is a cornucopia of fantasy and adventure where everyone can live in a child's make-believe world.

Bottom right **lovely Mission San Carlos Borromeo de Carmelo.** *Bottom left* **the Getty Museum. In Pacific Grove can be seen Green Gables Inn** *left.* *Below and facing page above San Simeon on "The Enchanted Hill" stands the domain created by William Randolph Hearst.* *Overleaf, left* **Death Valley.** *Overleaf, right* **the scene beheld Zabriskie Point.**

The coastline of California is at its rugged best along Big Sur, Monterey County. Waves roll against the rocks *top left* as the sun sinks into Pacific seas. In the Pebble Beach area, the famous golf course there provides wonderful sport, especially at the 7th hole *left and above. Top* a silver sheen sparkles from the waters at Bixby Creek Bridge. *Facing page: top right* deserted Garra Pata Creek. *Bottom right* Monterey daytime mist hazes the horizon where the blue of the sky and sea give way to land of undulating green. *Left* the sun sets in gold over Monterey Harbor. *Overleaf, left* Lone Cypress at Sunset Point; *right* Gray Whale Cove.

The Pebble Beach area of the Monterey Peninsula is one of outstanding beauty. Here there are three famous golf courses, each near to ocean and forest: Spyglass Hill, Cypress Point *facing page* and Pebble Beach *above*, its sixth and seventh holes observed from the air.

Overleaf, left on Highway 1, along the coast, is Bixby Creek Bridge. *Overleaf, right* a sun-shot mist clings to the Californian coastline, whose rock-studded shallows have proved to be the ruin of many a vessel bound for safe anchorage in Monterey Bay.

Golden Gate Park, San Francisco, is a tribute to William Hall – the first park engineer – and Superintendent John McLaren, who helped to tame 3 miles of shifting sand dunes to create the tranquillity and graceful beauty that is there today. It is an impressive park with many attractions, including the Buddha statue *right* and the Japanese Tea Gardens *below*. *Far right* mighty redwoods, ancient beyond the span of mortal man's years, straddle a footpath in Muir Woods National Monument.

Facing page: looking south from Mission Dolores Park lies the predominantly Latin area, with Downtown San Francisco dominating the skyline.

Dusk descends and the daytime workers in San Fransico's Downtown region bustle homewards. *Above and facing page, left* Powell Street undulates upwards to the historic heights of Nob Hill. *Facing page, right* the sun has bleached out all color to black and white.

Overleaf, left the friendly glow of living-room lights shines out from flat-topped buildings, above which the luminous, pyramidal spike of the Transamerica Building soars into the Californian sky. *Overleaf, right* cars scurry homeward across the Golden Gate Bridge, as dusk empurples the city scene.

Claiming to be the most crooked street in the world, Lombard Street *this page* changes direction ten times as it snakes past well-tended gardens on Russian Hill, between Hyde and Leavenworth.

Facing page: **Grant Avenue** is a very busy, but narrow thoroughfare bisecting Chinatown from north to south. The colors and odors permeate the senses with a feel of the Orient as one strolls along the sidewalk in this vibrant area.

Succulent and tempting, these displays of fish and roasted duck hang in the shop windows of Chinatown. The evening will bring many people here to sample the delights of tasty Chinese cuisine in restaurants set amid the atmospheric streets.

Overleaf, left **Fisherman's Wharf.** *Overleaf, right* **the Golden Gate Bridge.**

Although not as elegant as its older brother, the Oakland Bridge, with its two tiers of traffic, is equally indispensable, the silver monster carrying a far greater volume of vehicles which would previously have had to cross the bay by ferry.

San Francisco is the only city in the world with a cable car system in current operation *left and top.* Crawling along, the cable cars still carry up to 25,000 passengers a day in summer. *Facing page:* the contrast between old and new buildings in the city.

Frozen moments in time: a jogger *left* is caught by the camera's eye in mid-stride on the brow of the hill; justice being dispensed *above* and boarding the cable car *top*. *Facing page:* time is stretched as a long exposure records the signature of the car lights.

Previous pages **power and sail race over the sweep of shimmering sea or mist-shrouded waters.**

This page **a cobweb of latticework against the pastel evening sky, the steel cables, girders and massive pillars of the Golden Gate Bridge trace their way across the bay. A burning ball of flame** *bottom* **stains the scene a reddish hue with a gilded path over the waters. A lone yacht** *facing page* **sails homewards over a sea of silver, the silhouetted and rocky headland safely passed by to port.**

Now a tourist attraction, Alcatraz *top right* once housed the nation's most notorious criminals. *Top and above:* Oakland and Golden Gate bridges provide an essential link with the rest of California. *Right:* A forest of masts in Sausalito. *Facing page:* The marina.

This page: the Napa Valley, just north of San Francisco, produces fine grapes *above* and is synonymous with "The Wine Country". The huge casks *below* are in the winery of the Christian Brothers. *Left* traditional architectural style of the region set among magnificent surroundings.

The Napa Valley *above* is in the very heart of Californian wine country. Come September and golden October these vineyards will be ripe for harvesting.

Above **Junction Ridge, Kings Canyon National Park, in all
its massive grandeur. At the end of Yosemite Valley
cascades Bridalveil Falls** *facing page*. **It impresses not
through size or power but by sheer spectacular beauty, set
as it is among graceful domes and granite cliffs.**

Tenaya Canyon *facing page* **still bears the scars of Nature's glacial might which eons ago split the rocks and scoured the gorge. The still and quiet Mirror Lake** *above* **echoes the squat bulk of Mount Watkins.**

Described by naturalist John Muir as a "Range of Light",
the Sierra Nevada *these pages* is the largest single chain
of mountains in the country. An electric blue stream of
melt water *above* plunges irresistibly downwards. *Right* a
cerulean lake ringed by remnants of winter's icy grip.

These pages **Old Sacramento.** *Above* **2nd Street at dusk.**
Facing page **night scene.** *Overleaf, right* **the Capitol**
Building in Sacramento and *overleaf, left* **the magnificent**
rotunda.

Hat Creek *above* rushes between verdant banks through Lassen Volcanic National Park. An uprooted tree in mid-stream is etched by the constant flow of the water in flood. Isolated trees do find a foothold, however, in the lava beds *facing page* known as the "Painted Dunes".

Volcanic Lassen Peak *above* **looks down upon ice-blotched Lake Helen. Bumpass Hell** *facing page* **in Lassen Volcanic National Park still displays the action of geological forces as sulphur pools, boiling mud pots and clouds of steam vent from the volatile earth.**

Emerald Bay *facing page* **lies near the south end of Lake Tahoe, the "Jewel of the Sierra", which is 22 miles long by 8 to 12 miles wide, offering space and sport for all.** *Above* **a pool of bubbling mud in Lassen Volcanic National Park's Bumpass Hell.**

It is not only the giant sequoias that should be seen in
Sequoia National Park but also Monarch Lakes, Rainbow
Mountain and Mineral Peak *above*. *Facing page:* the lonely
magnificence of Columbine Lake and Lost Canyon.

Below: **Blue mist in Lady Bird Johnson Grove, Redwood National Park, California.** *Facing page:* **coastal fog over redwoods at sunset, California.**

Portland *these pages*, the "City of Roses", stands near the junction of the Columbia and Willamette Rivers and is dominated by the towering, snow-capped bulk of Mount St. Helens *above*.

As the largest, indeed the only, metropolitan city in Oregon, Portland *these pages* is the industrial, economic and cultural center of the state. Within the suburbs, which spread out around the city center, live some 850,000 people; nearly half of the state's population.

Oregon is famous for its scenic mountains and Mount Bachelor *facing page* **is
one of the most majestic. A chairlift ascends to the summit** *previous pages,
left* **from which can be seen views of the Three Sisters and Broken Top** *above
and previous pages, right.*

The high slopes of the mountains in Oregon ensure good skiing slopes for most of the year. Sunrise Lodge *facing page* **is a popular venue on the slopes of Mount Bachelor, whose Summit Chairlift can be seen** *above*.

Above **the Warm Springs Indian Reservation. The distinctive State Capitol** *facing page* **in Salem was built in 1937 and dominates Capitol Mall.**

Crater Lake *these pages* **is in the southeast of the state and is nearly 2,000 feet deep. Conical Wizard Island stands some 700 feet clear of the water and is a majestic sight at any time of the year.**

Overleaf, left **Eagle Crags above Crater Lake and** *overleaf, right* **Crater Lake Lodge.**

The incredibly blue Crater Lake, Oregon *these pages,* is something of a mystery. There is no inlet and outlet of water; no waterfalls fill it and no streams drain it, yet the snow and rain are in perfect balance with evaporation. There has been only the slightest variation in the total volume through the years it has been measured. Many volcanic crater lakes exist in the world, but none quite like this.

Previous pages, left **a view south from the Ecola State Park and** *right* **the Yaquina Bay Bridge, Newport. The coast of Oregon at Cape Kiwanda** *left* **and Yaquina Head** *top left*. **The Latourel** *above*, **Wahkeena** *facing page, left* **and Multnomah** *facing page, right* **Falls are all in the Columbia River Gorge.** *Overleaf: left* **Warm Springs River and** *right* **the Sahalie Falls.**

Above **Nahalem Bay seen from Oswald West State Park. Oswald West was Governor of Oregon from 1911 until 1915 and was committed to saving the beautiful Oregon coastline for posterity.** *Facing page* **the view south from Ecola State Park.**

Overleaf, left **the Columbia River Gorge and** *right* **Saddle Mountain.**

The rugged scenery of Smith Rock State Park *these pages* **is among the most dramatic in the state. Through the Park, which lies north of Bend, winds the Crooked River** *above*, **which drains into Lake Chinook.**

The peaks of the Olympic Range turn to varying shades of blue and purple in the twilight across Great Bend, on the Hood Canal *left.* **Dwarfed by the massive landscape through which it flows on its way to meet Snake River, is Palouse River** *above.*

The Space Needle *facing page* **in Seattle** *these pages and overleaf* **towers
some 600 feet above the ground and offers marvellous views of the city's
scenic setting, which is one of the finest in the country.**

Sculpted by the elements, the remains of a once mighty tree *above* lies on Rialto Beach, in the scenic wilderness of Olympic National Park, where the boat *facing page* skims across the sunlit surface of the Hood Canal.

Overleaf: generations of large-scale wheat growers have contributed to the manicured look of mile upon mile of the rich Palouse farmland *left*. Shown *right* is Picture Lake in the Northern Cascades.

Extending across Washington State from north to south, paralleling the Columbia River, is the Cascade mountain range *above*. The late sun illuminates the face of Mount Chuksan *facing page* as clouds drift below the summit.

Overleaf: between the blue of the flowers and the deeper blue of the sky, Mount Rainier *left*, in Mount Rainier National Park, rises to a height of 14,410 feet. *Right* Mount Adams, in the southern part of Washington State.

The volcanic nature of the Pacific Northwest is never far from sight. Mount St. Helens *facing page* in Washington erupted with a deafening roar on May 18, 1980, devastating over 150 square miles of forest. *Above* the aftermath at Spirit Lake.

Spokane, at the far eastern end of the state, was the venue of Expo '74, for which the U.S. Pavilion *above* was built. Coulee Dam *facing page* is the world's largest gravity-type concrete dam and has more generating potential than any other American hydro-electric scheme.

Overleaf the Peace Arch on the Washington-Canada border.